A Thousand Paths to Happiness

A Thousand Paths to

happiness

Sourcebooks, Inc.
Naperville, IL

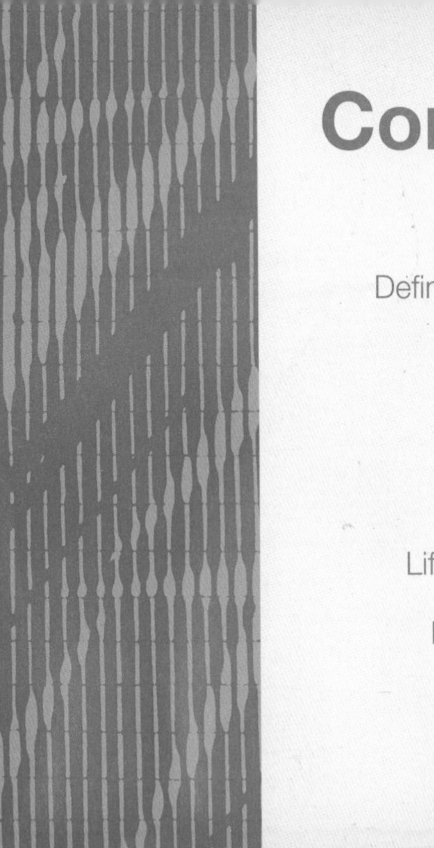

Contents

Introduction

Happiness is a state of mind which we must take control of for ourselves, and deciding to be happy can be as simple as tossing a coin in the air and saying: "Heads I'll be happy, tails I'll be unhappy!" The unhappiness that we fear is often not deep-rooted but simply the flip-side to happiness—we must allow ourselves the freedom to accept that unhappiness and happiness can live quite contentedly together at the same time and place. Like that coin, the thoughts contained in these pages will hopefully provide the inspiration for you to make the positive decision to choose happiness.

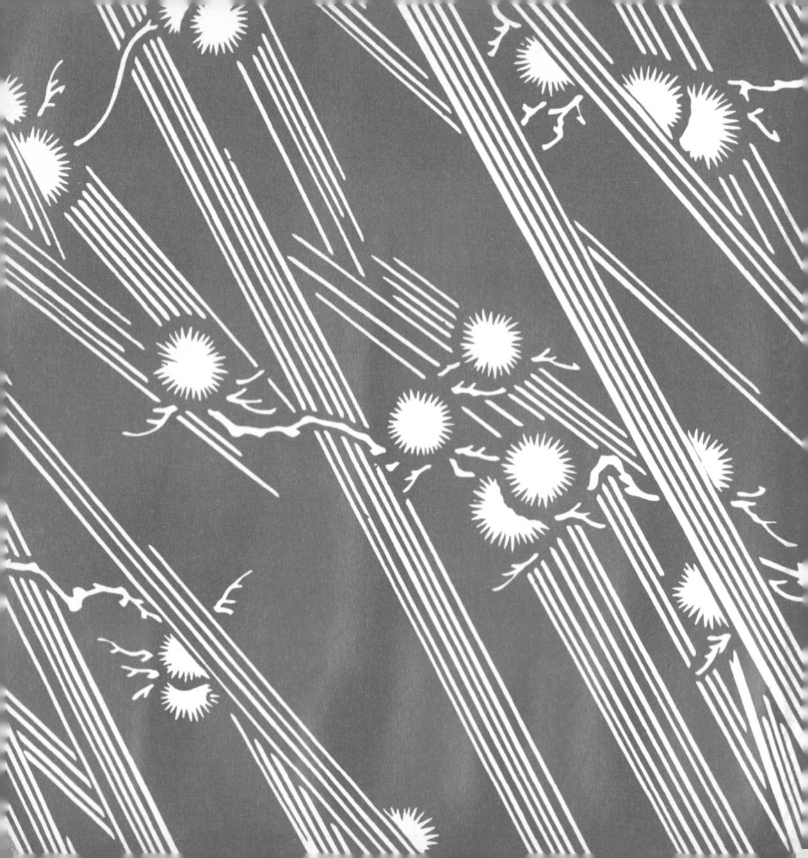

Defining Happiness

The moment you commit yourself to allowing happiness into your life it will be followed by a string of events that otherwise would not have happened, as providence comes into play.

Happiness cannot be found by following other people.
Find your own way.

There is no wrong time for happiness.

Happiness does not
depend upon getting
other people's
approval—
it depends upon
getting your own
approval.

Man worries...it is our natural state. We fear the future, are rarely content with what has passed, and dread death.

Experience your unhappiness while you've got it, you might never be unhappy again!

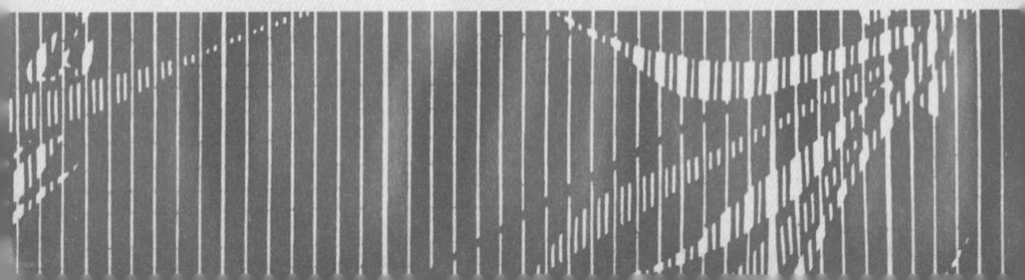

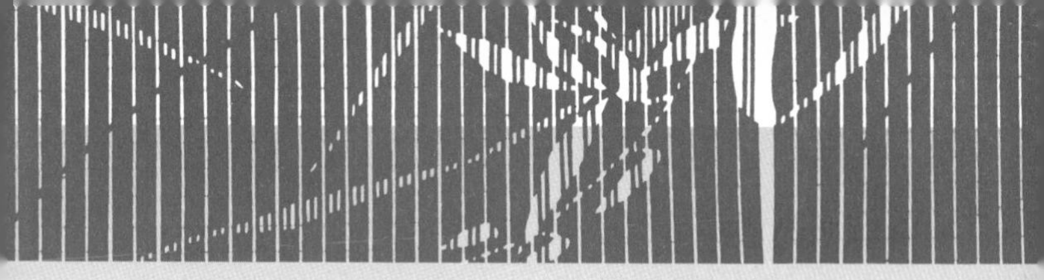

The path to happiness can be found by taking a good long laugh...at yourself.

The world will not devote itself to making you happy.

Finding your own happiness is like finding the source of a great river that has been dammed up by others trying to make you happy.

Happiness can come free and unexpectedly —don't seek it too desperately. Relax and it will appear.

Happiness lies in becoming unafraid of change.

Think of happiness as a kind of mental gardening.

Happiness is in the warm summer sun…

…in the red leaves of fall

...is near you when your light is low

...is there on the
autumn breeze

...it's on the warm wind

...is near you when your
faith is dry.

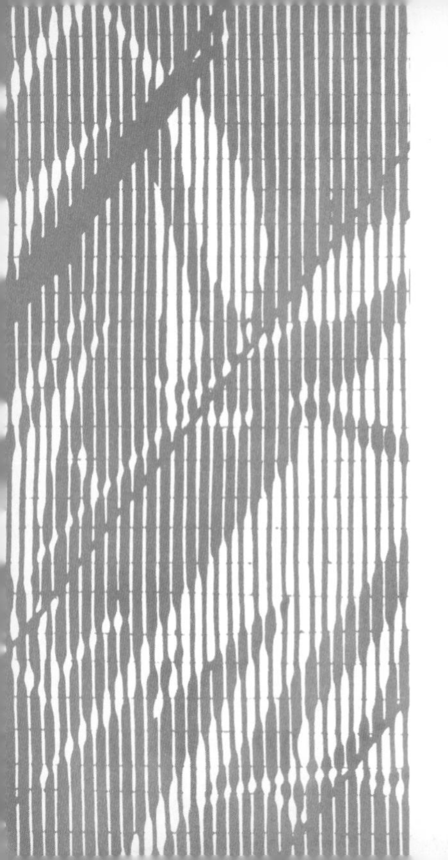

Happiness
is being
someone
—not
something.

The happy person often walks, unshaken, along the path that a thousand unhappy people insist is wrong.

Happiness is not about public opinion.

Happiness lies in putting off ’til the day after tomorrow what you can do tomorrow!

Happiness can be found in other people’s words. But not in being forced to speak them yourself.

There's no happiness to be found in tyranny.

Think of fear as a grain of sand and joy as the highest mountain.

Happiness is far too important a thing to be wasted by critics, cynics, and the quarrelsome.

If you are ready to reject aggression, revenge, and retaliation you are ready to be happy.

There is happiness to be gained from being able to accept that there are some things that cannot be changed.

The very fact that we chose to be what we are, despite wishing to be other, can cause our unhappiness.

Unhappiness comes when stubbornness leaves us trying to prove that there's no need to change our mind when we are given the choice to change our mind.

Happiness, like harmony in music, is when all your being comes together in complete agreement for even an instant.

Happiness' path is paved with your dreams and desires—down this path lies creativity, love, and long life.

A happy moment soon dies and never returns in an identical form. But that doesn't mean there aren't equally happy moments ahead—just new ones.

Don't squander your happiness in empty words—it is to be treasured, happiness is exciting, enthusiastic and magnificent.

There is no greater happiness than going out of your way to do something for a good cause in which your part is only discovered by chance.

The path to happiness can be found by doing as much good as you can by all the means you can.

No person can ever know what lies behind your happiness.

Happiness is the best adventure on earth!

Happy is he who has
intellectual curiosity.

Try to find happiness with as many different people as you can.

Now is the time to be happy.
This is the place to be happy.

The path to happiness may be paved with tranquil solitude.

Feeling you should be happy when everything inside you is telling you to be unhappy is like trying to correct nature —be unhappy and patient and happiness will come later.

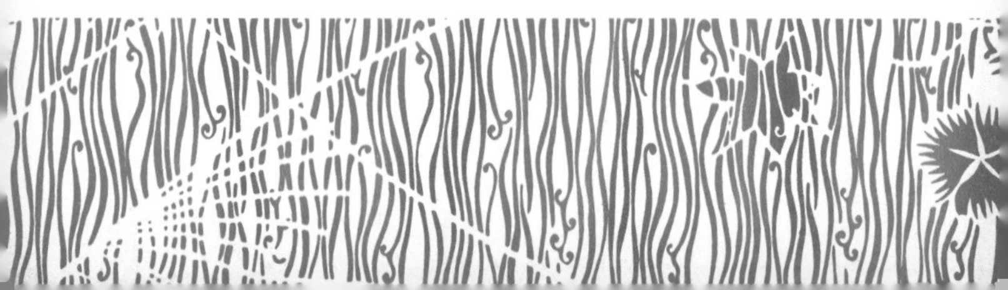

You don't have to fight or struggle to gain happiness.

Happiness lies along the path where our minds desire what the situation demands.

Sometimes you have to coax happiness like it was a child, reassuringly, carefully, lovingly, step by step.

You'll be happier thinking your own thoughts than trying to think other people's thoughts.

You can't always be happy with those things which are supposed to make you happy.

You want to feel good, you shouldn't feel bad about that. You want to be healthy and happy, you shouldn't feel bad about that either.

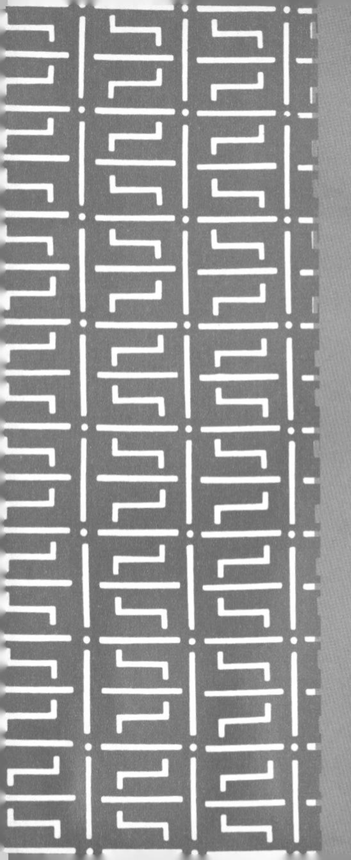

If you can forgive yourself for the mistakes you make, you will find true happiness.

It may sound strange, but it is possible to be happy about the fact that you are unhappy.

Is the grief and black despair in the winter rain, or in those who insist on seeing it that way?

Unhappy people usually carry some reason for unhappiness with them. Just in case one can't be found along the way.

Happiness is the flip side to every unhappiness.

Happy thoughts are powerful healers.

Love can turn sorrow to happiness.

The sweetest tears are the tears of happiness.

Happiness is in the smell of the coffee—rarely the taste.

Happiness is like a fig. You can't enjoy it before it's grown!

Happiness is like the goose that laid the golden eggs. You can enjoy happiness as it is freely given, or attempt to get too much, too soon, and destroy the source.

Some see happiness as superfluous
but as Voltaire said:
The superfluous is a very
necessary thing.

**Happiness is a much
underrated duty.**

Count on your fingers and toes
all the ways you can be happy.

**Hear yourself say:
"I am content."**

Develop the ability to get yourself to do what needs doing when it needs to be done—whether you like it or not—and you will find happiness.

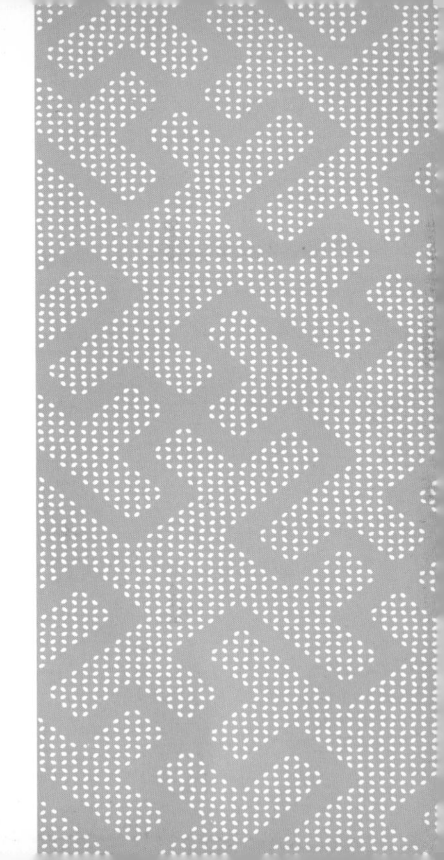

Find happiness with friends who are wise, quiet, and good.

In being happy, allow others some credit for your successes.

Happiness is being able to grow, develop, and share love and life.

Those that seem happy to others are not as happy as those who seem happy to themselves.

Happiness is unconditional.

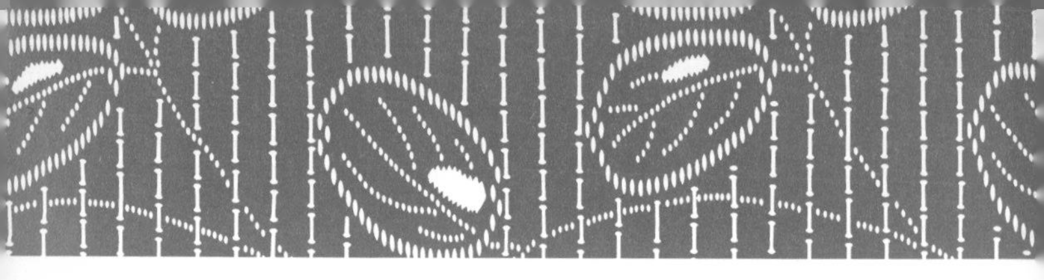

Happiness is always being able to acknowledge that I am enough just the way I am now.

You are certainly worthy of happiness.

Think of unhappiness as nothing but an old cave—and don't go in!

Adjust to your moments
of unhappiness and your
happiness will survive.

Discovering happiness is like bursting into the clearing from a dark and eery wood.

You cannot be happy when you are filled with envy and hatred. Wish well upon everyone equally and they will see you in a different light.

A smile can disarm many situations—
love and happiness are the stronger
enemies of conflict.

Bring a ray of happiness into other people's lives, and feel its warmth reflected back into your own.

Don't hoard your happiness.
Give it freely and you'll receive
even more than you gave.

The happier you are with others, the happier you will be with yourself.

In *Peter Pan*, flight was within the grasp of those who possessed a happy thought.

Happiness has the transforming power to free us from the pains and burdens of life.

Happiness is always there, underneath the anger and despair.

Happiness loves to happen.

Happiness sees you.
Can you see happiness?

The problem with happiness is that it is too often linked to the behavior of others.

Perhaps we are unhappy most of the time because we only grasp the happiness that we can understand.

Happiness might look small in your hands but let it go and you'll realize what a big thing it actually was.

Happiness is in the anticipation during the journey—not in the arrival.

Often the key to happiness gets mislaid—but the door is always unlocked.

Happiness waits patiently, like the night's desire for tomorrow.

Trying to understand happiness is like trying to understand something as vast as the universe.

As the American poet Robert Frost said, what happiness lacks in length it makes up for in height.

The peculiar thing about happiness is that when it is offered one distrusts it, then when it arrives it is enjoyed before it is believed in.

Think of unhappiness as a season which will pass, bringing sunshine and flowers.

If you fear losing happiness then you must have some happiness to lose!

Happiness is the best hedge there is against inflation.

Happiness is misfortunes avoided.

Happy people don't whine about their condition, or lie awake at night worrying about their duty or their sins.

You can find happiness in the brushstrokes of Michelangelo or underfoot on the lawn...

...you can find it carried on the air, and formed in the clouds overhead

…you can find it in
the dim light of each
new day

…you can find it in
the first frosts of
winter and in the
clear, pure voices of
the birds.

**Happiness
leads none
of us by the
same route.**

It takes two to be happy.
One to be happy and another to
witness your happiness.

Happiness lies in the achievement of happiness.

It takes no exceptional qualities to be a happy person.

Do not believe in happiness.
Know happiness.

Happiness and unhappiness is the stuff of life. Only some have more of it than others.

Happiness can make even familiar acts seem beautiful.

Material success does not lead the way to happiness.

Don't search for perfect happiness. Happiness is perfection itself.

Happy moments
follow each other like
lemmings—
so aim away from
the cliff!

Happiness is like a flower under the snow.

When the sun shines in your heart the beam can be seen on your face.

Happiness can be a secret place—somewhere to go to in your hour of pain, where a moment's peace can fill your heart.

A true heart is a happy heart.

Happiness to a child is lemonade, bunk beds, and a wigwam. Unhappiness is geography and double maths!

Happiness is bigger than any bank account.

Whenever there is love in your heart there is happiness in your life.

Happiness is a shelter in the storm.

Think of peace and find happiness.

Why be happy?
Because you're special.

Contentment is a form of happiness that goes beyond the senses of taste, smell, sound, and vision.

Happiness is rather like jazz. If you have to ask what it is, you'll probably never know.

Advice

A happy mind can do what wealth, medicine, and authority cannot.

What you are thinking now is contributing to the outcome of your life. So control those negative thoughts.

It is human nature to try out daring new methods. If they fail, they fail. Admit it. Move on to try something else, the important thing is that you never give up.

The biggest step
toward happiness
is through wisdom
and comes by
conquering fear.
Fear breeds cruelty
and superstition—an
unhappy blend.

As soon
as you
recognize
that you
are able to
control
your
thoughts
happiness
will come
within your
reach.

The worst enemy of happiness is fear.

Don't get bogged down by inconvenience. There's never a convenient time for happiness or unhappiness.

The less you complain about your grievances—the faster they will heal.

Tolerate and be happy.

Consider your energy and use it wisely.

Be heard—speak less.

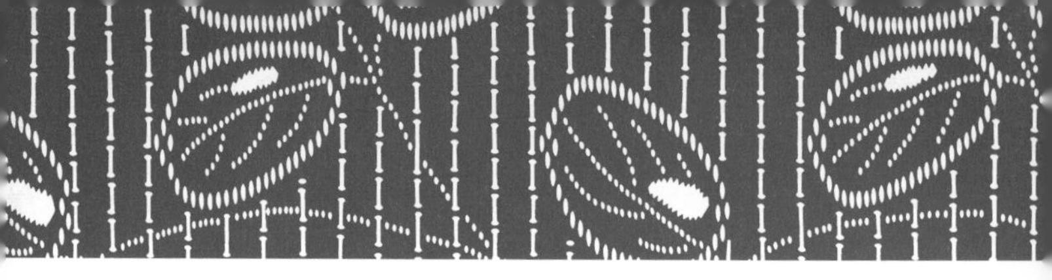

Allow yourself to be yourself—you can never be happy in someone else's shoes.

Try doing the thing it is that you think you cannot do.

Do not let fear stop you from achieving the thing you desire.

By all means pray for happiness—but don't forget to lend the gods a hand!

Imagine getting past the point of fear and saying “I stared at fear fully in the face and got through it and I’m ready to take anything else that life has to throw at me!”

Try to begin
things you feel
you can do.
To begin is
enough—there
is a boldness
in beginning.
And in boldness
lies genius
and magic.

There is happiness to be gained from finding the courage to change things that should be changed.

For something called "common" sense, why is there so little of it around?

If you can love your work you can be happy in life.

Turn your unhappiness into a mystery and enjoy trying to solve it.

Yesterday there was grief and today there is hope, tomorrow anything is possible.

Sometimes problems have to be faced from different angles in order to find solutions.

Lying is just a way of hiding from the truth.

Recognize yourself as a force of nature to be reckoned with.

Don't let the little things tie you down. Keep the wider perspective in your view.

Joy is the greatest weapon in the war against fear.

Be realistic about the problems you can tackle. Be happy in your decision and do not even attempt to do the impossible thing.

Happiness is like honesty. Beware of those who tell you they are honest.

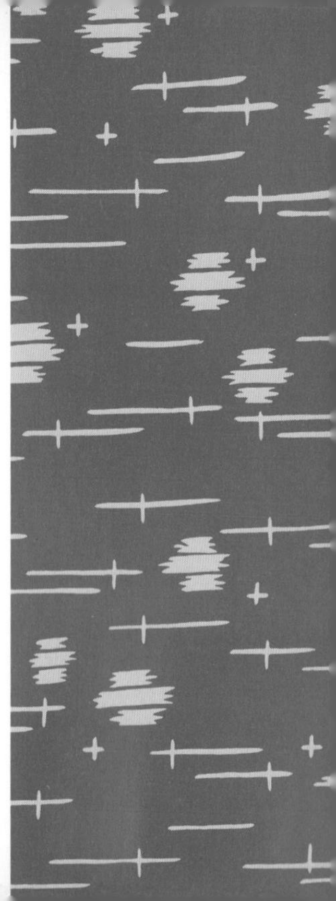

There is real happiness to be gained from being able to distinguish between things that cannot be changed and things that should be changed.

Live your life according to the light that is within you—or burn out.

We are taught in life that we should love our neighbor—just be careful where you build your house.

Spread your happiness around—don't place all your eggs in one basket.

Write down your unhappiness in a journal and save it for a moment when you feel strong enough to confront it.

The only failure is in no longer trying.

If your fear makes you unhappy, then try to do the things you fear—a fear conquered is happiness obtained.

There is more happiness to be gained by pleasing a friend, than from a friend's ability to please us.

You will never be a failure when you are capable of enjoying life—that should be the quest.

Do not let public opinion affect your happiness. Public opinion is built on little more than prejudice, folly, and weakness.

Better the happily impossible than the unhappy possibility.

If you have two doors in your home or room make the conscious decision each day to go out through the happy door or the unhappy door!
"Do I go out through the happy door or the unhappy door?"
Start the day that way.

Life is happiness defined in a word.

Do not let anyone tell you that you don't deserve to be happy. Happiness is the prerogative of all.

Assure yourself. It is within your own power, your own strength, your own energy, to find happiness.

When confronted by a serious issue do you hear yourself saying “They should do something about that!” Haven’t you realized that “They” is actually you?

Do go out looking for happiness. Forget your inhibitions and rediscover life.

Unite all that is you, your spirit, your heart, your body and concentrate all that you are on the happiness you want.

A child can turn nothing at all into absolutely everything, and unhappiness to happiness.

Hope is okay for breakfast but never as a late night snack before going to bed.

To truly gain your independence you must realize that on this earth we are all dependent upon each other.

Seek happiness in friendship—no person is useless if they have even a single friend.

Happiness is feeling that the world needs your work.

The best medicines in life can be found in a faithful friend or a happy moment.

Happiness is knowing you've got somebody to talk to.

Don’t worry about your entire future—it can only arrive one day at a time.

If you try to move a thousand bricks at once it will be impossible—but say to yourself “I can move that pile and do so easily a few at a time.” So is perseverance rewarded with happiness. Little by little.

There are as many inspirations to be had in the bath as there are in a cathedral.

Get used to a different way of looking at things. A change in perspective brings a whole new world of opportunity.

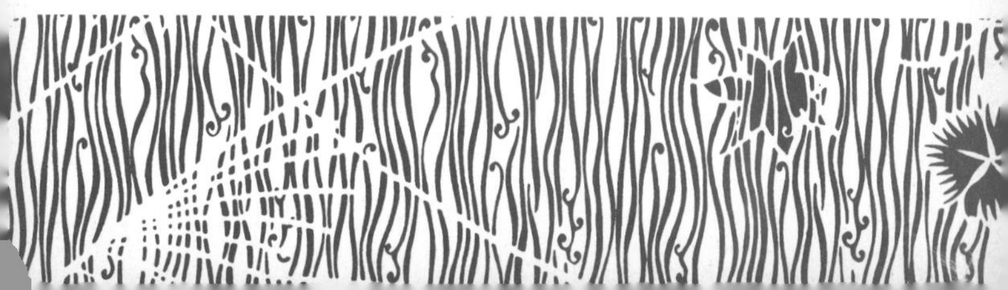

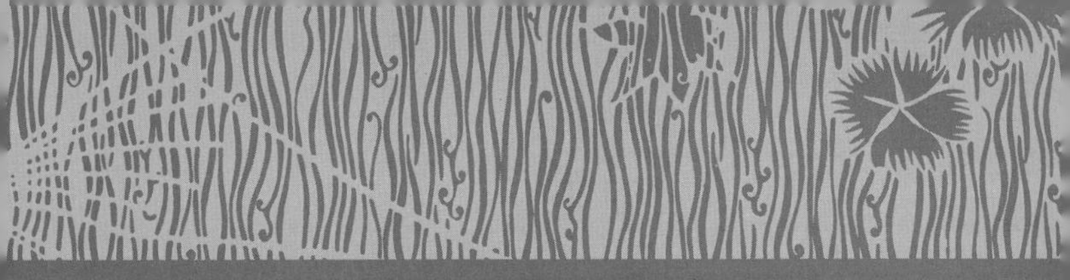

If at first you don't succeed, you are probably running about average.

To begin the dreaded task is to be half way to the happy goal of finishing it!

It will do you no good arguing with the inevitable. Relax, accept, and be happy.

Trying to hide unhappiness is like trying to hide gluttony. Impossible.

Do not waste time trying to bring disagreeable people around to liking you.

Don't blame circumstances for your unhappiness—but do look for the circumstances to create happiness.

You might consider yourself slow off the mark in the race toward happiness, but remember, even the sloth made it on board the ark!

Thoughts are as precious as water in a desert. Do not waste them on negativity—be refreshed, think positive.

Be careful what you wish for—you might be sorry when your wish is granted!

Try to be happy with yourself the way you are now.

Are you ready to accept the responsibility that comes with happiness?

Learn to trust in yourself. Then you will be ready to understand how to live.

Happiness won't be found by demolishing your entire house to rid it of a few wasps.

No matter who or what has wronged you, it is meaningless if you chose not to remember it.

Prepare for the long gloomy days of winter. Work put in during the pleasant season will pay off during the frosty spells.

Happiness is knowing that you have the courage to endure.

Don't burden yourself with anger for your enemies. Forgive them. That'll make them really angry!

Always take care of yourself, then you will always be ready to take care of others.

Be your own best friend.

Be true to your inner self. Like the tree, stand fast against good fortune or bad. Neither fair weather nor foul can shake it.

You must try to become the person you would like to spend the rest of your life with.

Remember: Nothing outside of you can upset your inner happiness.

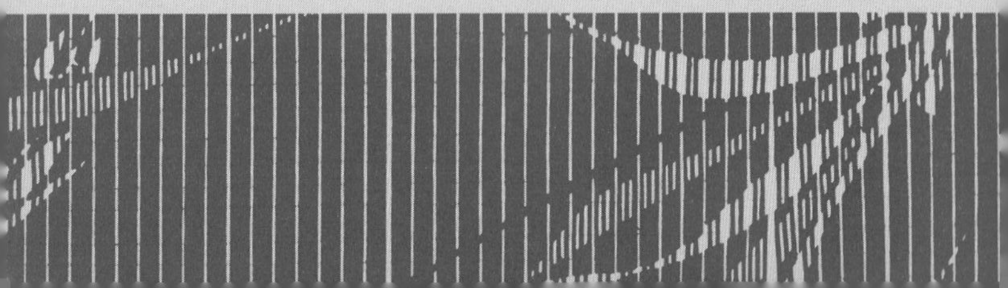

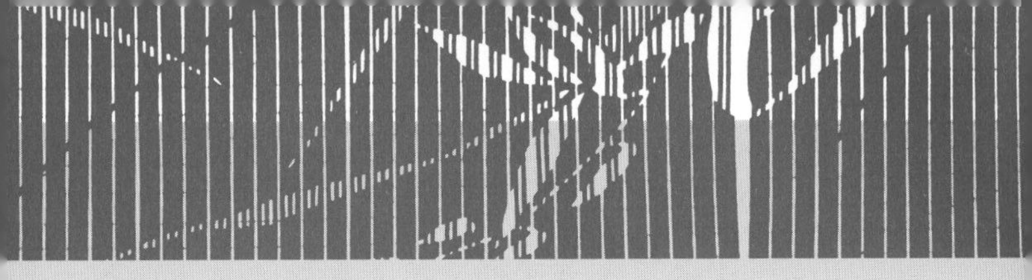

Unhappiness is turbulent waters, and, like the sea, the turbulence will pass and the water will become calm again.

Free up your energy to create a peaceful, happy life.

Every moment is the ideal time to embark upon the path to happiness.

Try to go through a moment in the day without wanting or not wanting.

Try to go through a moment in the day when you care and don't care equally.

Find your place in the flow of things and remain still...you will succeed.

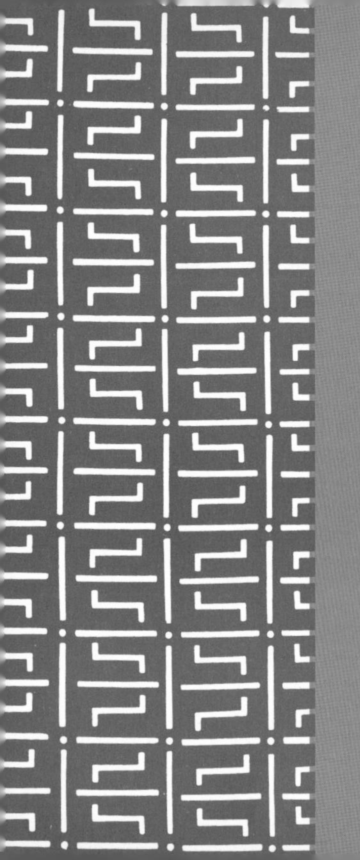

Devote your energy to happiness, energy spent worrying is wasted energy.

Take happiness as it comes,
and don't wish for more than
you are given.

Imagine the happiness of knowing
that you do not necessarily require
happiness.

The things you like and the things you dislike can drive you mad if you think about them too much.

Think of solitude as a kind of partner.

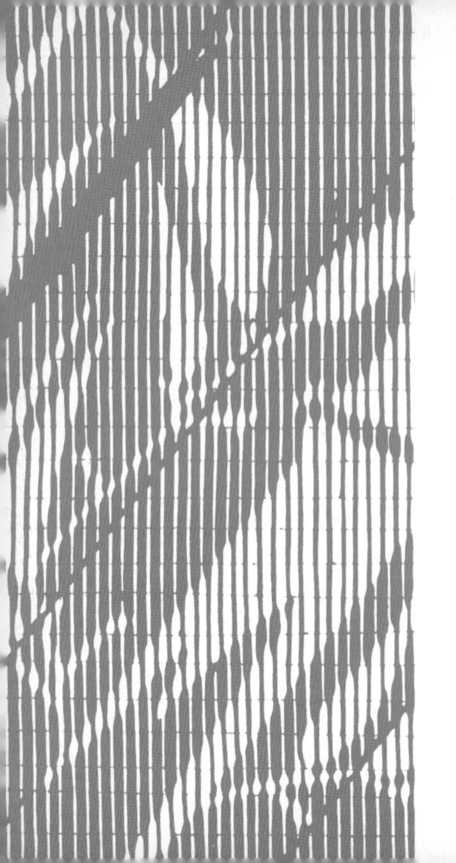

Allow yourself to turn your thoughts away from the physical things that surround you and look in on yourself.

Try to sleep as if for the very first time.

Sometimes, in order to open your eyes to the possibilities of today, you have to close your eyes on yesterday.

Teachers open the door but you must enter by yourself.

Try to wake as if for the first time, and see the world through fresh eyes.

Don't go to great lengths in your search for happiness. Great happiness can be found in small ways.

Think of love and be happy.

Happiness can't be found by trying to please everybody all of the time. If you can accept that, there is hope for success.

Find your WHY and the HOWS won't matter any more.

Your cheerfulness can do wonders for others as well as yourself.

Put your smile on someone else's face!

A happy person puts the news in the postscript.

Chose your moment and feel alive for that moment.

A halo doesn't go with everything and is just something else to worry about losing.

The worst lies you can tell are the ones you tell in silence.

Don't place all your happiness into something that can be stolen or broken.

Try to follow your own advice before you offer it to others.

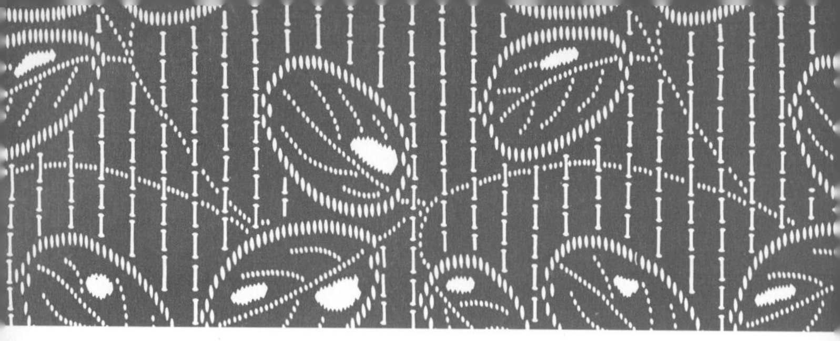

Sometimes you have to look through the wrong end of the telescope.

Try doing the thing it is that you think you cannot do. Prove yourself wrong.

Allow yourself some time in your day to be alone with yourself.

Feeling impatient is wasted energy. Learn to understand the reason for the delay and relax—anger won't speed things along.

Sometimes it's uplifting to read someone else's thoughts—they have a way of implanting themselves into your memory and are capable of providing good thoughts.

Make the decision to allow happiness to come to you.

You can draw away from happiness, hesitate, or simply be too busy to notice it. Or you can grab the moment and commit yourself to allowing happiness into your life.

Happy conversation is like good music —it has the ability to reach into the deepest corners of your soul and to provide all manner of cures.

Can you honestly feel that you have more right to a happy life than anyone else?

Love and luck and happiness take a great deal of hard work.

Change and the world will change with you.

Happiness costs nothing and is worth so much.

The battle without can never be won if you lose the war within yourself.

Honesty has the power to destroy fear.

Try to admire without envy.

Don't base your happiness for the future on some happiness in the distant past. Learn to love the present.

Don’t sit around taking your chances with destiny. Make your choice and see if you can achieve it.

Work

There are no problems that can't be faced. Experience, knowledge, and confidence tell us how they should be approached.

If you have a good mind, be prepared to use it well.

Hope, enterprise, and change go hand in hand with happiness.

The most important person you can ever get to know is yourself—so get networking.

You look and ask "Why?"
Try to look and ask "Why not?"

At the end of our lifetimes we know nothing—in youth we know everything.

Making the decision to begin something could be the beginning of something great.

Time is money. Stop wasting money.
Time is life. Stop wasting life.

Sometimes you have to be prepared to start anew.

We all have the potential of enormous energy.

In this life there are far fewer "possibilities" for experts.

There must be something in your day that you would be happy to achieve.

Unhappiness comes from constantly debating the outcomes of things that can't possibly be controlled.

The one thing that you can rely upon
is that truth breeds truth.

Something that explains everything
in the end will explain nothing at all.

Be blithe, be brave but most of all
be happy.

Turn your doubt over from time to time.

Be patient and happiness shall satisfy you.

We have an explanation for everything
but know nothing.

Happy work is greeted with a kindlier hand.

Don't blame yourself for overestimating yourself. Reassess and go again.

Mind your own business.

Try not to analyze everything. Analysis kills happiness.

Sometimes you'd think the end of the world had come—it hasn't.

One moment of bliss can obliterate countless numbers of hours of pain.

It's no good sitting around remembering when you were happy. Be happy.

Next time you feel the door to happiness has closed before you, remember it has only done that in order that another door to other happiness can open.

Think seriously about the environment and do some small thing to help it. We cannot live happy, healthy lives in an unhealthy world.

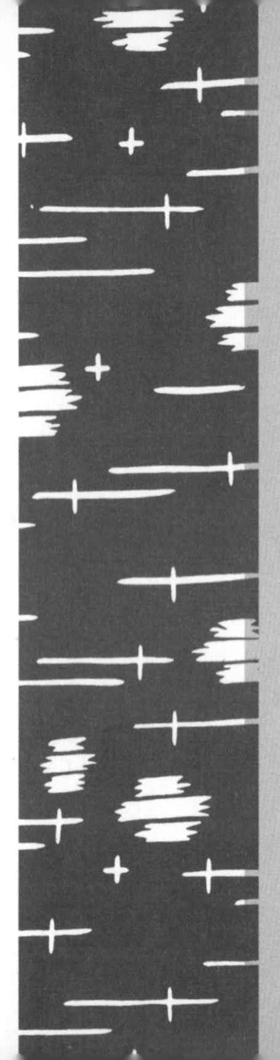

Be sure that no one is going to pull the rug from under you when you jump for joy.

Experts are a health hazard.

Listen. Your heart will tell you the reasons for joy.

Lose the badness of your badness and the sadness of your sadness. Rediscover the gladness of your gladness.

Work can be seen as the "grand cure" of all the miseries of mankind.

Anyone who can laugh heartily at themselves has found the way to happiness.

Remember the acorn—mighty things from small beginnings grow.

Humility wins cooperation and respect.

How is it some people seem to do everything they do with such ease, and for others the smallest action is a supreme effort?

Beware the fury of a patient man.

What do we all seek?
To live at ease, and not be bound to think.

Call today your own and live for today!

Say a thing well and it will be remembered—and so too will you.

Try and still your mind. Now.

Concentrate your attention—or risk mistake.

It is of no use to lock yourself away with yourself if you are not prepared to accept that it is you that makes you unhappy.

You can't kill time without injuring eternity.

Try asking without smiling:
"Why is this thus? What is the reason
of this thusness?"

Friendship rarely brings money—
that is the job of business.

Leave time and room in your life to accept change.

Are old friends the people you like the best—or simply the ones that you met first?

If you intend to live for a very long life, you had better be prepared to be honest—or have a very good memory.

Those who seem to disagree with everyone else's opinion always have plenty of their own.

Finding solutions through argument is as easy as constructing a boat out of rice paper.

Give yourself credit for knowing more than you think you do.

Try to pray for something that is not a miracle.

Avoid being criticized for your mistakes by acknowledging them as soon as they occur.

Beware of naked emperors.

Work can banish boredom, vice, and poverty—and therefore unhappiness.

Think of unhappiness as a bad job and resign.

How often do the teams working on happy and hopeful projects succumb to obstacles, and in time, abandon all hope and with it their happiness.

Are you happy to oblige?

Don't
let
your
anger
keep
you
poor.

If you are unhappy with the way something is dragging on bring it to a speedy end.

The greatest quality is the quality to sustain happiness in the light of adversity.

Regain your authority, and with it your happiness.

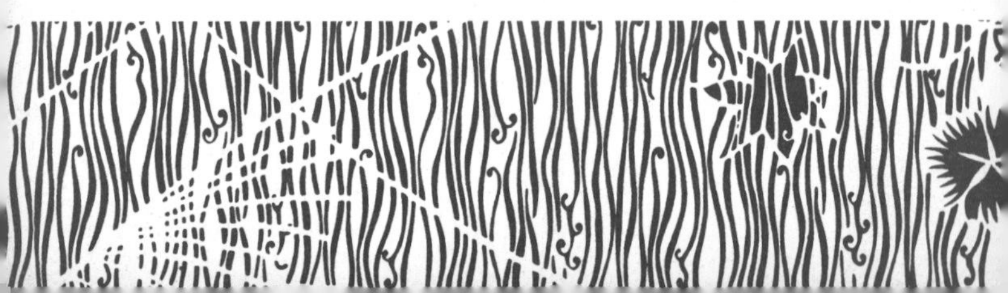

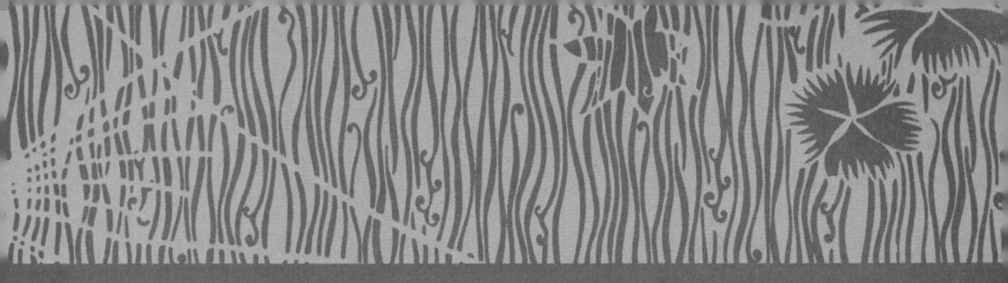

I haven't got the time to stop (for happiness).

You cannot drink from a coconut before it has grown.

Consider the consequences of your actions before you start anything.

Tap into the force of happiness.

Success is an unreliable measure for happiness—it is quite possible to be successfully unhappy.

There are more great people throughout history remembered for their hour of trial than for their triumphs.

Help yourself to help yourself.

Avoid those who tell you:
"You can't do that—if it was worth doing someone would have done it by now."

There are two kinds of truths. There is the truth that is acceptable to you, and the truth that is acceptable to liars.

You can be the creator of the moment.

Will happiness come with wealth or wealth come with happiness?

To succeed, you must be happy in the decision that the price of your desired power might be your liberty.

Open yourself to the possibility of discovering solutions.

Create precedents don't just follow them.

There is only one thing you cannot do to excess and that is be charitable.

You may be powerful enough to control an army but have you the power to control yourself?

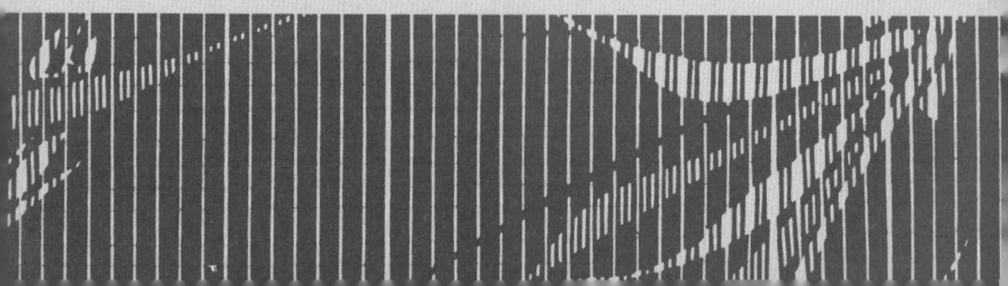

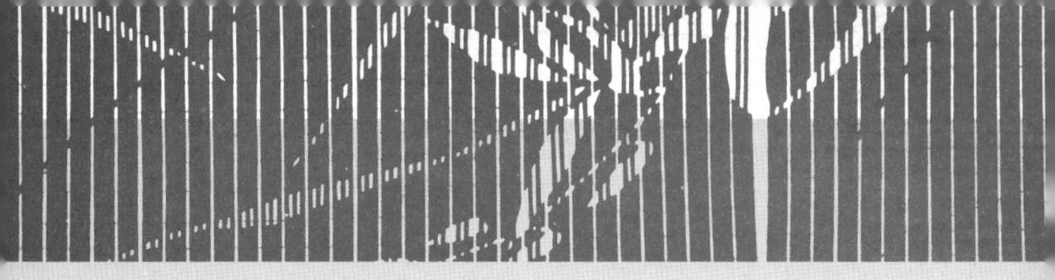

In this life nothing great is ever achieved without enthusiasm.

You might very well be bold—but can you keep your promises?

To be great you must be prepared to be misunderstood.

You can either look for opportunities—or make them.

To have failed in business is hailed as a brave misfortune, but to fail at life is seen as recklessness.

Success is being able to distinguish between what are your lies and your truths.

Knowing the price of everything and the value of nothing—that will not bring happiness.

The optimist turns problems into opportunities. The pessimist turns opportunities into problems.

Happiness is being able to rename your mistakes as experience.

Try showing enthusiasm towards others who are successful around you—can you do it sincerely?

Work is either well done or badly done.

You can either get there morally or immorally. Happily or unhappily.

Tread lightly on other people's dreams.

Nobody can do more than their best—it may not always be enough but there can be no regrets.

One moment in life you fear the fact that people might be talking about you and the next, you're devastated if they are not.

Be careful in your choice of enemies.

Work is the curse of the idle.

Stand out from the crowd—put on a smile.

A man may leave behind him his works—therein lies his talent. But he takes with him his life—therein lies his genius.

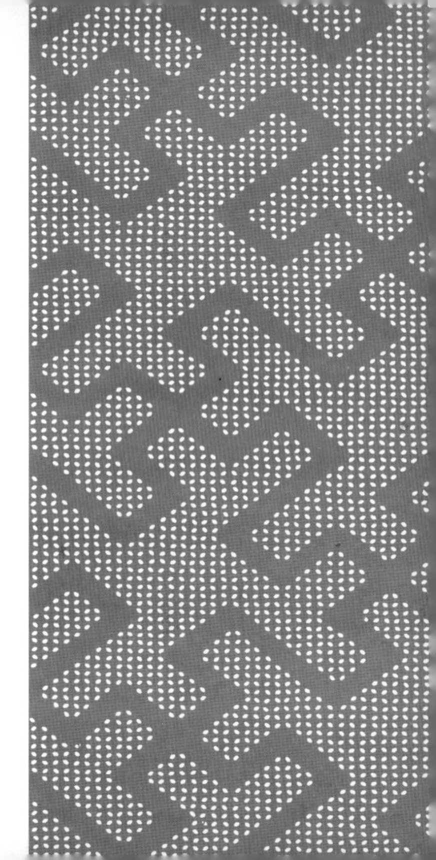

To find happiness in life you must be prepared to accept that sometimes your best will not be good enough—but it's better than if you'd done nothing at all.

Think of your problems as a challenge in a game you enjoy playing.

Sometimes you have to be prepared to give in for respect to show itself.

Sometimes you have to face difficulty with a smile to overcome it.

There is little to compare with the happiness that comes from the results of your efforts.

Sometimes you can quell anger in others by listening to what they have to say.

Think of peace and find happiness.

Deflect anger with happiness.

Don't minimize your contribution.

You can't build a relationship based upon falsehood any more than you can build a hang-glider from margarine.

Sincerity breeds confidence.

No task is too difficult to perform—it is only thinking that makes it so.

Your honesty will produce as much satisfaction for you as it will for others.

You can never hope to know what the future holds if you don't even know what to do next.

You should not expect thanks for something done with love as it will bring about its own rewards.

Let every action that comes toward you have a positive and creative reaction from you.

Act naturally.

Fortune, fame, praise, and power are as destructive to their dependents as defamation and insults.

Task plus love equals success.

There are more solutions to be found in calmness than in turmoil.

Plan carefully and consider each step.

Try taking pleasure in the tasks you perform.

Surprises in life can be exhilarating but surprises in planned schemes can terrify.

Your happiness can make others less afraid.

Suspicion and assumption are the hands that will pull the rug out from under you.

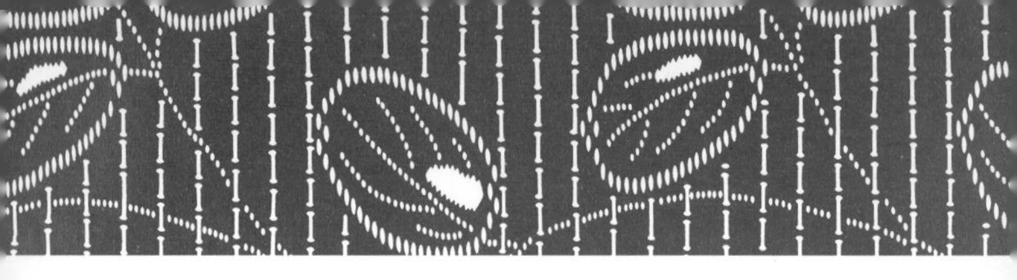

Every morning
dedicate a moment
to yourself and your
place in the new day.

Mood

Be happy to explore your potential. Most people live in a very restricted circle of their potential being and use only a small portion of their resources.

Learn to avoid those things that make you feel restless.

Allow yourself to make your own decisions.

Optimism is the ability to perceive evil only where it exists.

I **will** make time to do the things I enjoy doing.

I **will** learn to relax.

I **will** improve my skills.

I **will** learn to say no.

I **will** learn to delegate responsibility.

Happy
people
tend not
to suffer
from
stress.

It is impossible to separate the diseases of our physical being from the cause and effect of the heart and intellect.

Laughter is a better medicine than any doctor can prescribe.

Allow yourself the luxury of time to get through bouts of unhappiness.

Learn to recognize your tendencies toward unhappiness—if you can, you will be able to control them.

Happiness begets happiness.

Happy people are, in general, calm people.

Prepare yourself for good dreams and avoid things likely to give you nightmares.

Work to improve your memory—concentrate more and pay attention to detail.

Happiness takes root and spreads.

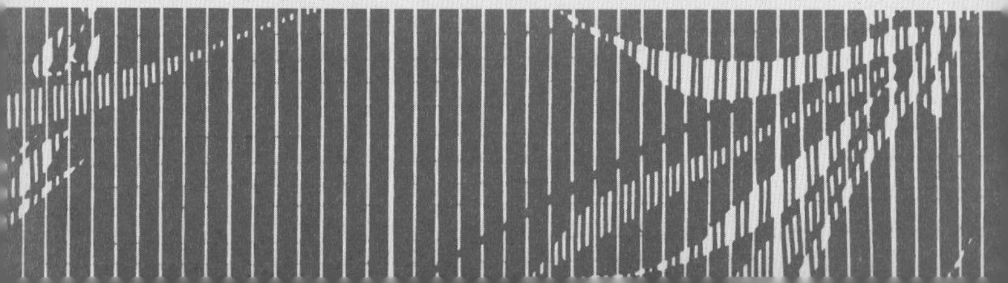

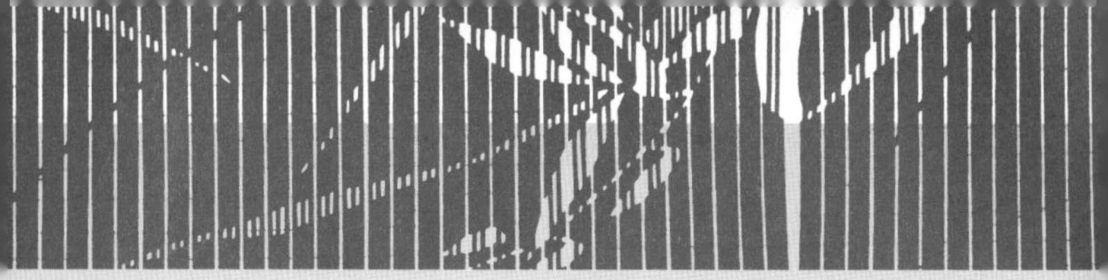

Step over the little things that make you feel nervous.

Unhappiness devours all things.

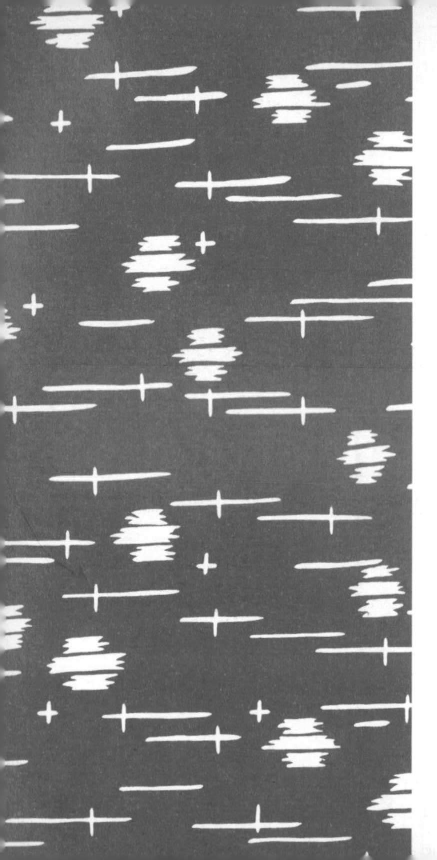

Happy people always seem to have good energy.

When you find your thoughts racing, put the brakes on and think one thing through, or do a jigsaw puzzle.

We all have an equal share in possibility.

Recognize the importance of "play" in your life. It is essential to give yourself dedicated time to unwind.

Try to avoid bouts of sudden irritability—periods of moodiness can close the door to happiness.

Work to curb any impulsive behavior before it has the chance to get out of control.

There are more choices for the happy person.

Don’t panic about anything. Keep calm.

Happiness is never out of fashion.

Cry if you feel the need. A good cry can often clear the air.

Those who are happy tend to share their feelings more than others.

Don't be influenced by external pressures. Start to value yourself for who you are and what you are. No more. No less.

When you feel you can't do very much about something, do everything you can.

It is impossible to be happy while you continue to smother yourself with the concrete blanket of indifference.

A happy heart can tame the strongest grief.

Success breeds success, and nothing shuts down motivation faster than failure.

If you accept the limits of human reason and life you will achieve a uniquely human kind of happiness.

Never take on so much work as to feel overburdened.

If there is anger around you and within you, you must allow yourself to express it, but guard against this becoming habit.

Don't allow the little things to overwhelm you.

Don't pace the floor, go out for a walk. Stretch your legs and fill your lungs.

Happiness can be found by doing something as simple as a yoga class.

Go to the park.

You can't feel accomplishment if you don't start something and complete it. Read a book, make a model, clean a mess, do a good deed.

Try meditation, alone, in pleasant surroundings.

Allow yourself to procrastinate from time to time for fun, but never as a way of avoiding serious issues.

If the pressure of time is making you feel stressed, take down the clock or don't wear your watch.

Try being early for a change—it's a buzz.

The happy man does not hear the clock strike.

Allow yourself to be organized—it may be all you need to find happiness.

Happiness lies in learning to be more assertive in your life.

Happy people look at things differently.

See your job as equivalent to that of any famous actor or performer. Be a star, go out and do your act and get paid for it.

Unhappy about your inability to handle more than one problem at a time? Prioritize and work your way through your list, leaving each completed task behind.

Find it hard to relax? Try something new—go out for breakfast or lunch and soak in the whole event—leave everything else behind for that time.

Happy people take their happiness seriously.

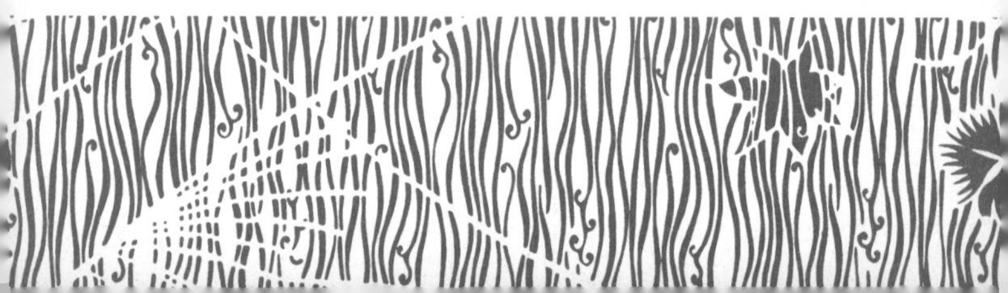

Positive thought and action are the enemies of sorrow.

Happiness will always find a way, no gates are locked to it.

Unhappy about facing a particular situation? Your unhappiness will remain as long as you avoid it. Imagine how happy you will be after facing up to the task—this may be all the catalyst you need.

Positive thought and action are the enemies of sorrow.

Sometimes a little change in your daily routine can provide happiness—anything from changing the color of your bath towel to taking a different route to work.

The happy person is rarely selfish. Joy multiplies.

Angry? If you are able to identify the source of the anger in your life you will be closer to happiness.

Happiness is feeling in control of time.

Put your worries or problems on ice overnight while you sleep.

Preplan to meet deadlines and always incorporate contingency time.

When real situations at work or home make you want to explode with anger or sink into unhappiness, say to yourself, “I’m glad this is only a game.”

Happy people have
little problem
speaking their minds.

You'll never find happiness if you don't allow yourself to express your feelings.

Wisdom is knowing
when to remain silent.

You'll be happier doing jobs you feel qualified to do. Do not feel the need to always over-reach yourself.

When something is beyond your capability instead of saying to yourself "I'm so stupid" try saying "Boy that's really something—imagine being able to defeat someone as great as me!"

Meet changes in your routine half way.

It is easier to be happy when you are not surrounded by the confusion and the clutter of life.

Draw up a list of things that you've always wanted to try and "go for it!"

Show me an unhappy gardener.

Try writing...a list, a letter, a journal, a novel, a declaration.

To be happy is above all bargains.

Happiness is the energy that turns the world.

False happiness fades with time—true happiness will last forever.

Unhappiness undermines us. There is no greater crime than destroying somebody's happiness—including your own.

Happiness cannot be harnessed like a horse—treat it gently, it cannot be forced.

Happy people can handle tense situations comfortably.

Bring your skills to the job.

Strive for happiness and win back your life.

Happy people have less need for routine.

Happy people have a quicker route to the subconscious and solutions to problems.

Happy people are positive people.

Happy people make the best friends.

Happy people are more open to change.

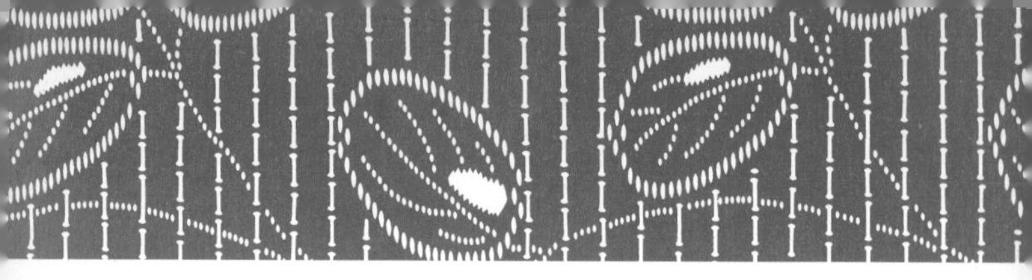

Read something that YOU want to read, not something that you feel compelled to read.

Labor is light where happiness pays the wage.

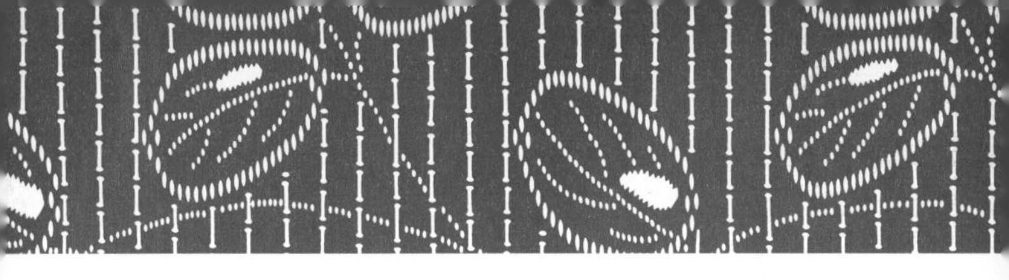

Happiness has no pecuniary value.

Happy people are more capable of controlling how much they take on and have no difficulty in saying "No."

Those who are happy get more
from every moment than those who
surrender to their sadness.

Is it possible for you to avoid some
of the things in life that make you
angry or unhappy altogether?
If so, do so.

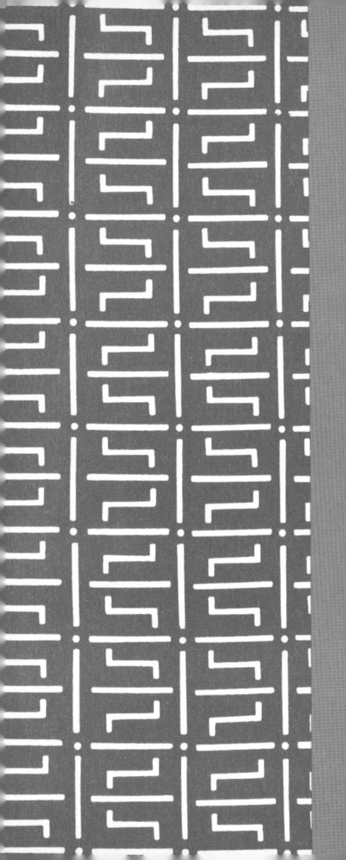

A happy face is the best letter of recommendation.

Those who are happy tend to have more influence.

Find happiness by scheduling quality time for yourself to do things that are unrelated to anything else that you do.

Happiness makes one fit for any work.

Every once in a while, take the opportunity to look around you, at the things that bring you joy. Do not take your happiness for granted.

Happiness is the unexpected bonus of a generous heart.

Where there is no trust there can be no happiness.

Try and avoid the things that over excite you easily, strive to achieve a more balanced environment.

Happiness is working around the flow of your energy, not someone else's.

One day of pleasure is worth several of sorrow—an ounce of mirth is worth a pound of misery.

Happiness is a great healer, sorrow is a terminal disease.

All men are equal in the eyes of happiness.

Happiness has the power to make even the hardest of hearts gentle.

The only romance that will last forever will be achieved when you can love yourself.

Unhappiness is a file that wears us down but makes no noise.

Don't let feelings of inadequacy take root, learn to be happy with yourself and others will follow.

Do you suffer from bouts of disorientation? Go to your favorite place for a walk

Do you become angry if you're made to wait? Look around and fix your thoughts on something else that has nothing to do with what you're waiting for.

Shared laughter is the best tonic.

Stop worrying. It is the best anti-aging treatment!

Relax, and let happiness find its way to you.

Whatever you do, don't withdraw yourself from other people.

Happiness is like a sneeze—neither can be contained.

If you suffer feelings of helplessness or frustration do something constructive...go and feed the birds in the park.

Happiness is stronger than fear.

Happiness comes through positive action, through setting and achieving your own goals. It needs no teaching.

Don't sit back and wait for happiness to happen.

Decide to be happy and you are half way there.

Life and Death

There is birth and there is death, two acts to a complex play called life and between them is an interval which should be enjoyed.

Don't forget to live sometime on your journey to the grave.

A happy thought is the greatest tonic.

Never take pleasure in the discomfort of others, nor take your own happiness too much for granted.

Do not grieve over the inevitable.

Embrace happiness.

Learn to value your happiness. Never turn your back on it.

Happiness is the greatest gift, accept it graciously.

It is easy to feel isolated in personal sadness. But remember, no sorrow is new—all mankind is linked by shared experience.

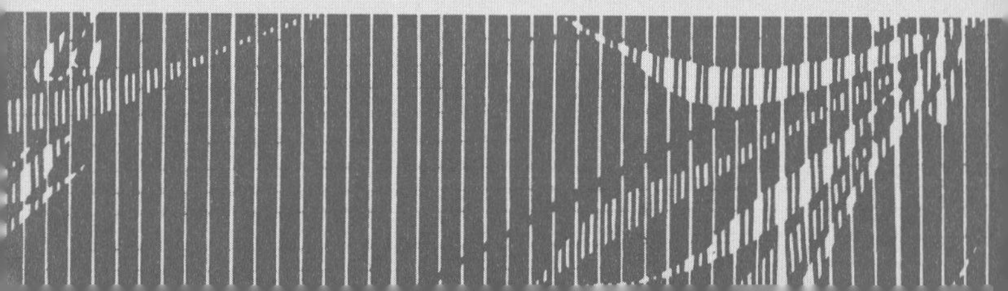

Try to be satisfied with what you have.

To dwell on unhappiness is a selfish act.

Happiness is doubled when there is someone to share it with.

Do not ground your happiness in material things. They are all too easily taken away.

Life is to be enjoyed.

Unhappiness is one of the consuming illnesses of our time.

Avoid falling into habit or you will cease to be.

Remember in life that you are never alone in your fight against unhappiness.

Thoughts not strength rule the world.

Wasting of time is wasting life.

Follow your desire for as long as you live.

Don't waste your energy envying others their happiness, they are probably busy envying yours.

The curious thing about human beings is the way we seem to actually worship our negative emotions.

How often can you hear yourself putting yourself down and expressing a low opinion of yourself to others, and yet how often have you told yourself that you don't deserve what you're going through?

Be honest with yourself, if you cannot accept yourself as you are, how can you expect others to?

Get involved—many of our illusions of unhappiness come through our detachment.

One of the rarest things to be discovered in life is truth.

Happiness loves to be elusive, and then take you by surprise.

The
greatest
happiness
is to allow
your heart
to become
as pure
and simple
as a child's
again.

Listen to what children have to say—their windows to the soul are unclouded.

When we are very young we are told that sitting still and keeping quiet equal good, and that running and laughing equal bad. Reverse those ideas.

As morning shows the day, so childhood shows the man.

Sometimes a helping hand is a frightening thing to be offered.

As Pubilius Syrus observed as far back as 1 B.C., the fear of death is more to be dreaded than death itself.

Is it death that you fear or not knowing "what" or "where" is after death?

The moment that you can accept the inevitability of your own death you will become free to live.

Who is the more miserable—
the person who goes through
life wishing he was dead
or the person who goes
through life fearing death?

Use your life for something you really believe in.

Just because you allow yourself to laugh doesn't mean that you take life any less seriously. Happiness relies on humor and a sense of perspective.

Ever noticed that people who live life deeply seem to have no fear of death?

The healing process requires a cocktail of time and opportunity which we must provide for ourselves.

Don’t waste time fearing death. It has not come yet, and when it does come we won’t be here to worry about it!

Where we “are” death is not, and when death does come we “are not.”

Death is just a good night’s sleep, a dream—whether it’s unconsciousness or nothingness or a crossing of the soul from this world to the next, the whole of eternity is but a single night.

Worrying about death is as futile as worrying about who will be coming to your funeral.

There is no subject that we contemplate more, and no subject that we have as little power to influence, than death.

Next time you stare into the heavens wondering whether there is life elsewhere in the universe, ponder too the possibility of your life on earth.

You're going to kick yourself for not realizing sooner what a wonderful life you have had!

There was a man who would check the newspaper everyday to see if his name was in the obituaries—then he would sigh with relief and enjoy each day as though it were his first and his last.

Don't worry about dying from an overdose of satisfaction.

When death comes, eventually, let it find you doing exactly what you want to do.

If you choose to live on a diet of hope, you are likely to starve to death.

Those who are unhappy about the thought of charity toward others are usually not charitable toward themselves.

Who says that you can't live the life you dream?

Look at life with a sense of humor, for as the wise man said, you'll never get out of it alive!

Make it your priority to enjoy life.

Mankind's interest in death is just another interesting way of looking at life.

The last thing you should intend to do in life is die.

A happy disposition is the best prescription for the ills of mankind.

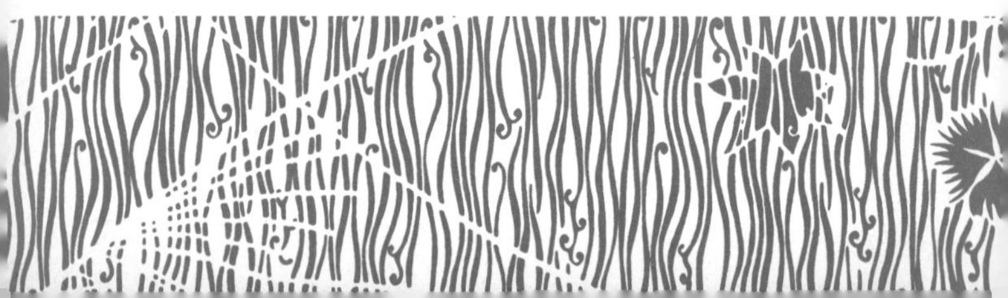

Life is rather like receiving acting lessons while you are on stage giving a public performance!

Mankind is strange—we attempt to control nature when we cannot even control ourselves.

You can't be happy living to the rule of yes and no if everything you say yes to is bad and everything you say no to is good.

We live one life, but inside us there are many possible lives—some happy and some unhappy. It can go either way depending upon what confronts us.

Human life must be dedicated to something. Happiness, your own or others, is as good a place to start as any.

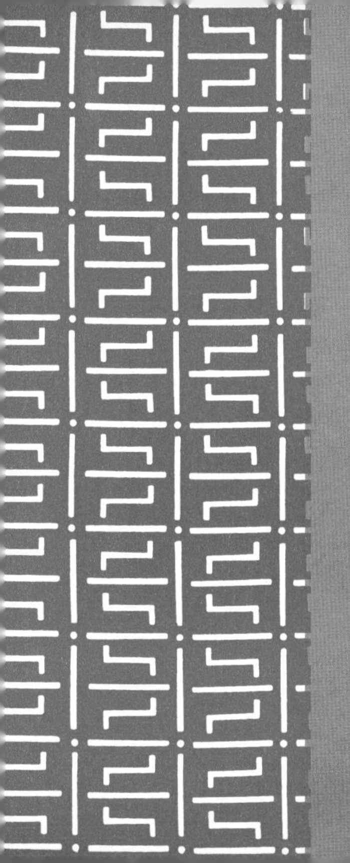

Unhappiness often lies in the mistaken belief that the limit of what we are able to perceive is the limit of all that there is to perceive.

Life is a riddle that we must learn to enjoy solving.

We all have an equal share in possibility.

Half the secret of happiness is recognizing how to let it proceed on its own without trying to force it.

Never feel guilty about your happiness. Life is short—seize joy where you can.

God grant me patience...now!

Try looking at the thing that makes you unhappy from a different angle —imagine if you could channel all the energy you expend on those negative feelings into making yourself feel better about yourself.

You can force a plant—regulate temperatures, water carefully, and control feeding—and the thing you plant will flower. OR you can patiently wait and watch and find as much happiness in those moments knowing that each is building toward a flowering to be enjoyed.

Life is to be enjoyed. Don't forget to smell the flowers as you go.

Allow all things to play their part, let the axe fall under its own weight, the blade to fall along the grain. No effort. Harmony.

On gloomy days, don't spend time looking for patches of blue. Instead, see the beauty in the clouds.

The search for happiness is like sowing a seed, it is an act of faith.

No one can be you better than you.

Everything belongs.

Balance the past, present, and future.

Don't worship the guide, but where it takes you.

The Zen approach to archery has the archer aiming at himself.

We are all distinctively the same.

Only fools go through life trying to make fools out of other people.

Treat your belief as your guide. Then, it will be yours and become part of your life.

I'd like, one day, to talk to the man who has lived so well that he has no need for words.

Through life you'll discover that happiness is to be found in what seems trivial, the everyday stuff of life—a falling leaf, snow, a fly.

I wish I were what I was when I wished I were what I am.

Happiness can show us how to see into the life of things and gain a glimpse of enlightenment.

On John Ruskin's desk there was a stone and on it was carved the word TODAY.

Place your trust in serendipity.

The world of childhood is so intense—try and recapture some of that urgency for living.

Be happy in the knowledge that you are not struggling in the world alone.

Why experience everything through another person when we can experience everything through ourselves.

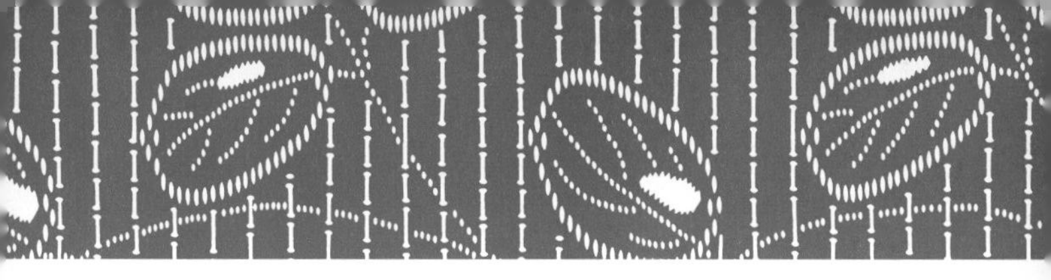

It's easy to be unhappy but there is usually a struggle for happiness!

Children are afraid of the dark for the same reason we fear death. It is simply fear of the unknown, not the thing itself.

Happiness is knowing that life is everlasting. Give yourself a pinch and feel everlastingness in the flesh.

The problem with humans is that we set ourselves up in lives that make happiness impossible to achieve and then sit there wishing we were happy instead of doing something about it.

Happy is he who is not weighed down by the stones of this life.

Instead of being quick to take anger, look for the positive in a situation—however hard it may seem. It is a habit that can save you unnecessary stress.

A happy person does not go through life living in dread of days to come.

Happiness is contagious—be careful who you sit next to!

The most important person for you to get to know is yourself.

Sorrow is often touched with joy.

We are all unique, but carry the same burdens of self-doubt, fear, anger, and grief.

It is easy to feel isolated in personal sadness, but remember, no sorrow is new.

It seems that man has ever striven for happiness, only to live in fear of losing it once he has found it.

The more you have in this life, the greater your chances of losing something.

It is quite possible to live without happiness—but where's the fun in that?

One of the most wonderful things to possess is knowledge of a life well-spent.

Many people in their pursuit of happiness seem only to make their lives more unhappy.

Find joy in the perfect balance of nature.

To dwell on unhappiness is a selfish act.

Do not dwell on things that cannot be altered. There is no profit in it.

Don't blame the past for making you unhappy, nor set conditions for future happiness. Stop and look around you. This is your life. Now. Enjoy.

Withdraw your opposition to
unhappiness and happiness will follow.

To find happiness you have to be
prepared to stimulate the mind.

Life is a thousand times too short for us
to bore ourselves.

There is no soul that crosses from this life untouched by happiness.

Those who speak ill of this world are usually those who have never succeeded in living in it.

The happy person knows that it is difficult to argue about color in the dark.

Why do we go through life so acutely aware of everybody else's happiness, and forget to appreciate our own?

There may be virtual reality, but there is no such thing as virtual happiness.

Are you struggling to get the shape of your life right, like a Hollywood script in the hope of an Oscar?

Everybody has the right to feel the way they feel—don't deny your emotions.

Happiness grounded on material things is happiness built on unstable foundations.

Happiness comes from recognizing that the greatest loss in life is actually what we allow to die within us while we live—not death itself.

Philosophies

Different men seek after happiness in different ways and by different means and so make for themselves different modes of life and forms of government.

Aristotle

Your joy is your sorrow unmasked and the selfsame well from which your laughter rises was oftentimes filled with your tears.

Kahlil Gibran

One man's metaphysics is another man's primrose.

Philosophy is a kind of journey, ever learning yet never arriving at the ideal perfection of truth.

Albert Pike

A peasant and a philosopher may be equally satisfied, but not equally happy. Happiness consists in the multiplicity of agreeable consciousness.

Samuel Johnson

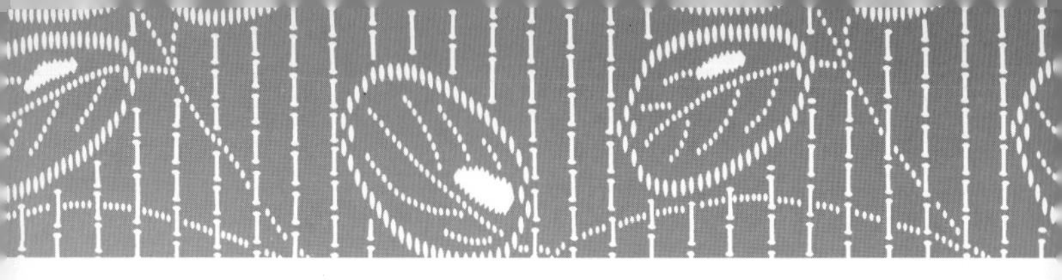

We are long before we are convinced that happiness is never to be found, and each believes it possessed by others, to keep alive the hope of obtaining it for himself.

Samuel Johnson

What's the use of worrying?
It never was worthwhile,
So, pack up your troubles in your old kit-bag,
And smile, smile, smile.

George Asa

Though we travel the world over
to find the beautiful, we must
carry it with us or we find it not.

Ralph Waldo Emerson

I don't do anything that's bad for me. I don't like to be made nervous or angry. Any time you get upset it tears down your nervous system.

Mae West

Joy's smile is much more close to tears
than it is to laughter.

Victor Hugo

Thinking is an experimental dealing with small quantities of energy, just as a general moves miniature figures over a map before setting his troops in action.

Sigmund Freud

Laugh and the world laughs with you, weep and you weep alone.

E.W. Wilcox

Happiness is elusive—the moment we seem to enter the happiness state we begin to falter, like a horse refusing to jump a hurdle. Is it our fear of not achieving happiness or do we fear happiness itself?

One joy scatters a hundred griefs.

Chinese proverb

To fill the hour—that is happiness;
to fill the hour, and leave no crevice
for a repentance or an approval.

Ralph Waldo Emerson

The fight does not always
belong to the strong and the
swift do not always win the race.
But odds are the gambler will
always bet that way.

Damon Runyon

**Universal happiness keeps
the wheels steadily turning;
truth and beauty can't.**

Aldous Huxley

Most of the time we think we're sick,
it's all in the mind.

Thomas Wolfe

The mind is its own place, and in itself can make heaven of hell, a hell of heaven.

John Milton

Happiness lies in philosophy where the foolishness of yesterday becomes the wisdom of tomorrow.

All that is comes from the mind; it is based on the mind, it is fashioned by the mind.

The Pali Canon

There is perhaps nothing so bad and so dangerous in life as fear.

Jawaharlal Nehru

If I could drop dead right now, I'd be the happiest man alive!

Samuel Goldwyn

Pessimism is saying all's well when all's going badly—herein lies unhappiness. Optimism turns the same moments around by recognizing that all will be well after things have been going badly—herein lies happiness.

He is happy that knoweth not himself to be otherwise.

Thomas Fuller

To become the spectator of one's own life is to escape the suffering of life.

Oscar Wilde

Public opinion is a petrified forest where nothing grows—it's good for only one thing. Nothing.

Mirth is like a flash of lightning, that breaks through a gloom of clouds, and glitters for a moment; cheerfulness keeps up a kind of daylight in the mind, and fills it with a steady and perpetual serenity.

Joseph Addison

Everything is in your mind...the future...the past...your mind is capable of anything, even happiness. Don't let the little things tie you down. Keep the wider perspective in your view.

Neither a lofty degree of intelligence nor imagination nor both together go to the making of genius. Love, love, love, that is the soul of genius.

Wolfgang Amadeus Mozart

Not to be and not to have give an immeasurable freedom.

Janwillemvan de Wetering

Pleasure
is the
beginning
and end
of living
happily.

Epicurus

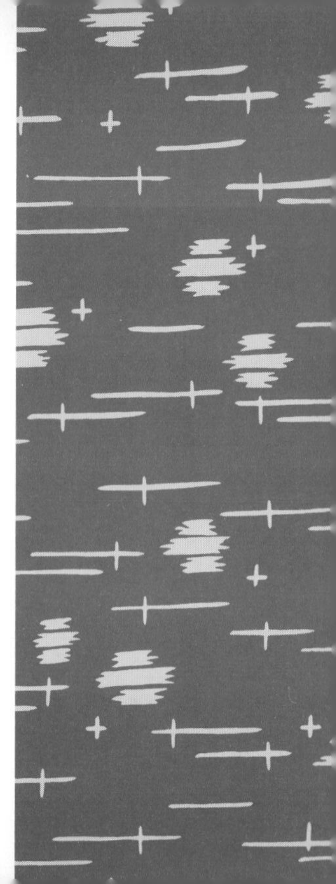

Think of unhappiness as a winter, the time of year seen as barren, but which is really the season that prepares for life, and gives birth to spring.

Gladness of heart is the life of man.

Apocrypha, Ecclesiasticus

The nature of happiness is a circle of which the center is everywhere and the circumference is nowhere.

Beware the emperor who is proud of
his new clothes simply because the
salesman tells him he should be.

A thing of beauty is a joy forever:
Its loveliness increases; it will never
Pass into nothingness.

John Keats

We should consider every day lost on
which we have not danced at least once.
And we should call every truth false which
was not accompanied by at least one laugh.

Friedrich Nietzsche

No matter how dull, or how mean, or how wise a man is, he feels that happiness is his indisputable right.

Helen Keller

Happiness is like a sunbeam, which the least shadow intercepts.

Chinese proverb

It seldom happens that any felicity comes so pure as not to be tempered and allayed by some mixture of sorrow.

Miguel de Cervantes

Catch life as it flows.

Unhappiness is sharpening it's scythe on the grindstone of your indifference.

Happiness lies in the fulfilment of the spirit through the body.

Cyril Connolly

Every day is a good day.

Happiness is a bookworm its belly full of thought...

Illusory joy is often worth more than genuine sorrow.

René Descartes

It is impossible to live a pleasant life without living wisely and well and justly and it is impossible to live wisely and well and justly without living pleasantly.

Epicurus

Happiness is brief
It will not stay
God batters at its sails

Euripides

A great obstacle to happiness is to anticipate too great a happiness.

Fontanel

True joy is the nearest which we have of heaven, it is the treasure of the soul, and therefore should be laid in a safe place, and nothing in this world is safe to place it in.

John Donne

Human felicity is produced not so much by great pieces of good fortune that seldom happen as by little advantages that occur every day.

Benjamin Franklin

You can try to convince yourself that wealth and success can create happiness, but the pleasure they supply is only a short-lived psychological condition, not real happiness. Real happiness comes from a life well-lived.

Croesus was surprised and angry and said “Man of Athens, dost thou count my happiness as nothing?” “In truth,” replied Solon, “I count no man happy until his death, for no man can know what the gods may have in store for him.”

It is tragic to think that one might die without ever hearing laughter—so laugh now, even before you are happy and perhaps happiness will follow.

Jean de La Bruyère

We hold these truths to be self-evident, that all men are created equal, that they are endowed by their Creator with certain unalienable Rights, that among these are Life, Liberty, and the pursuit of Happiness.

from the American Declaration of Independence

The seeds of unhappiness may be planted by too much pressure toward too many difficult new achievements.

Success in building skills upon early experience, depends most of all upon happiness.

Man's unhappiness, as I construe, comes of his greatness; it is because there is an infinite in him, which with all his cunning he cannot quite bury under the finite.

Sartor Resartus

Happiness is acceptance and friendship.

Effective communication is essential to a happy life. Feel free to talk about positive feelings of love, joy, and appreciation as well as negative feelings of anger, fear, and disappointment.

Time spent in creative activities such as music, art, hobbies, education, and community service are more condusive to happiness than passive recreations such as television, radio, and spectator sports.

Chess, like love, like music, has the power to make men happy.

Siegbert Tarrasch

Something as simple as the colors that surround us can influence our happiness. Warm colors like pink, rose, yellow, orange, and red have been proven to increase feelings of comfort, warmth, and happiness!

Freedom from pain in the body and from trouble in the mind is the goal of a happy life.

Epicurus

Man is the measure of all things.

Protagoras

While every pleasure is in itself good, not every pleasure is to be pursued because some pleasures may entail painful consequences that outweigh the pleasures themselves. The individual must learn to discriminate between pleasures that are really good and those that only seem to be good.

**Happiness is a gift of God,
not the result of pursuing virtue.**

Philo

To live well requires the exercise of practical wisdom—moderation, justice, and courage—to balance pleasures against pains and to accept, when necessary, those pains that lead to greater pleasures.

Pure and complete sorrow is as impossible as pure and complete joy.

Leo Tolstoy

Moderation in all things.

Weeping may endure for a night, but joy cometh in the morning.

Psalms 30:5

A man hath no better thing under the sun than to eat, and to drink and to be merry.

Ecclesiastes 8:15

We are so made that we can derive intense enjoyment from a contrast and very little from a state of things.

Sigmund Freud

The Indian religion Jainism states that in its pure state the soul possesses unlimited happiness, knowledge, perception, and power. But once entrapped in the human body, these faculties are contaminated by the senses, limited by location and space and subject to cause and effect, birth and death.

We have no reliable guarantee that the afterlife will be any less exasperating than this one, have we?

Noël Coward

Utopia, the Greek word for "nowhere," is the name of an imaginary island with a happy society, free from all cares, anxieties, and miseries.

Show me a sane man
and I will cure him for you.

Vincent Brome

Nothing can harm a good man, either in life or after death.

Socrates

Try to find happiness in history and you will find only crimes and misfortunes.

We keep passing unseen through little moments of other people's lives.

Robert M. Pirsig

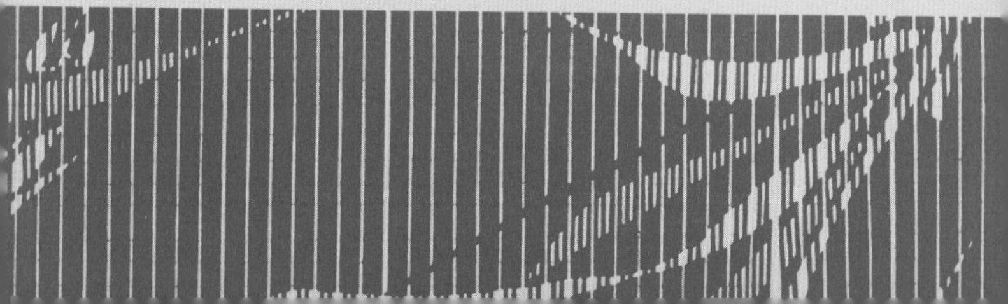

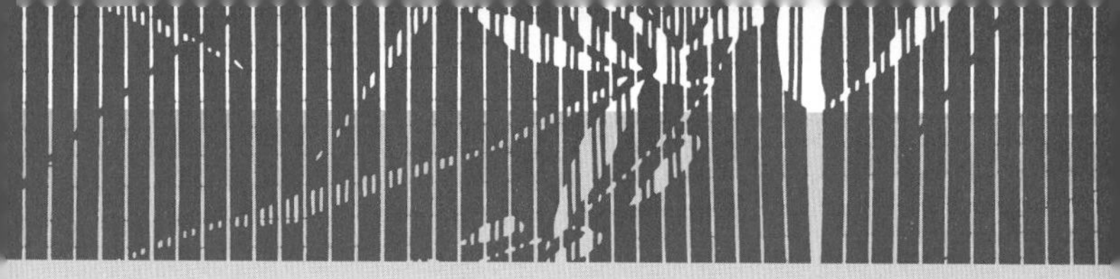

For in all adversity of fortune the worst sort of misery is to have been happy.

Boethius

A useless life is an early death.

You can learn how to learn but happiness comes to he who learns how to think.

My advice to you is not to inquire why or whither, but just enjoy your ice cream while it's on your plate—that's my philosophy.

Thornton Wilder

It's only thinking, so don't give it another thought.

The small share of happiness attainable by man exists only insofar as he is able to cease to think of himself.

Theodore Reik

So have I loitered my life away, reading books, looking at pictures, going to plays, hearing, thinking, writing on what pleased me best. I have wanted only one thing to make me happy, but wanting that, have wanted everything.

William Hazlitt

Democritus, known as the “Laughing Philosopher” proposed happiness, or “cheerfulness,” as the highest good—a condition to be achieved through moderation, tranquility, and freedom from fear.

I celebrate myself, and sing myself.

Walt Whitman

Poetry is the record of the best and happiest moments of the happiest and best minds.

Percy Bysshe Shelley

The value of eternal happiness is infinite and that although the probability of gaining such happiness by religion may be small it is infinitely greater than by any other course of human conduct or belief.

Blaise Pascal

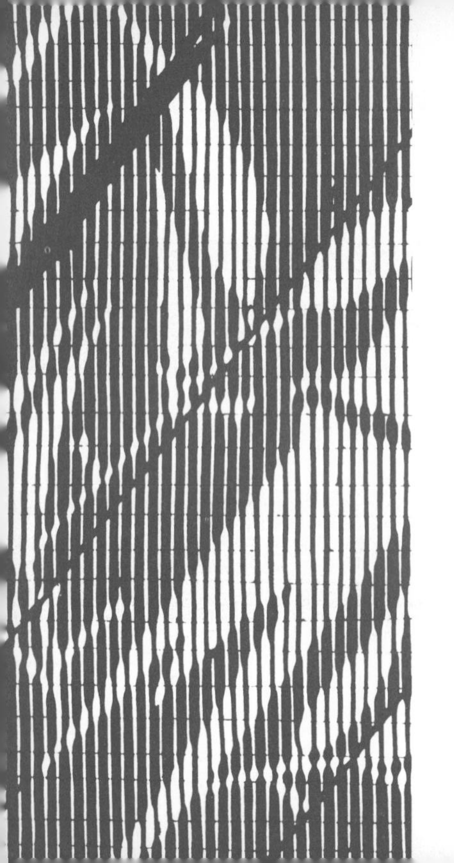

Correct actions are those that result in the greatest happiness for the greatest number of people.

Jeremy Bentham

Adversity has its hope. Prosperity has its fear.

The lies that are allowed to sink in do the most hurt.

If you can remember your troubles you can just as easily forget them—remember only happiness and your troubles will fade into the background.

Your happiness is as significant as a tree. Attempt to show me an insignificant tree and you will fail.

It is neither wealth nor splendor, but tranquility and occupation which give happiness.

Thomas Jefferson

Happiness does not grow in the garden of angry thoughts.

There's beauty all around our paths, if but our watchful eyes can trace it midst familiar things, and through their lowly guise.

Felicia Hemans

The stages of the Noble Path are: Right View, Right Thought, Right Speech, Right Behavior, Right Livelihood, Right Effort, Right Mindfulness, and Right Concentration.

Buddha

The power of happiness is the power of life.

Want of control over the senses is called the road to ruin; victory over them, the path to fortune. Go then by which way you please.

The Hitopadesa

Unselfish happiness is the key to everything.

Do not be afraid of showing your affection. Be warm and tender, thoughtful and affectionate. Men are more helped by sympathy, than by service; love is more than money, and a kind word will give more pleasure than a present.

Sir John Lubbock

What sunshine is to flowers, smiles are to humanity. They are but trifles, to be sure, but scattered along life's pathway, the good they do is inconceivable.

Joseph Addison

Happiness isn't won —it's deserved.

We are all shaped by the things that make us happy.

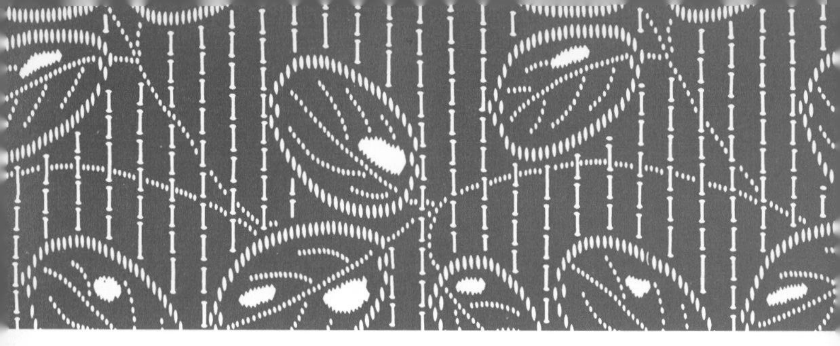

There is greater happiness to be found in taking steps forward for your own belief than for the belief of others.

I dreamed a thousand new paths…
I woke and walked my old one.

Chinese proverb

Happiness wins the battle
before it is fought.

The block of granite which was an obstacle in the path of the weak, becomes a stepping stone in the path of the strong.

Thomas Carlyle

Seek happiness through knowledge—without it, it's hard for anyone to get on in life. Try beginning with your own self-knowledge.

To bring up a child in the way he should go, travel that way yourself once in a while.

Josh Billings

We're told in life that our reach should not exceed our grasp and then we are told to look forward to heaven.

The results of an hour well-spent will live on forever but an hour lost is never regained.

If you spend your life worrying about losing happiness, you will neglect to enjoy what you have, when you have it.

Lord, make me an instrument of your peace. Where there is hatred let me sow love; where there is injury, pardon; where there is doubt, faith; where there is despair, hope; where there is darkness, light; and where there is sadness, joy.

St. Francis of Assisi

The tears you show on your face will soon dry but the tears of your soul are far more difficult to mop away.

Happiness is the only good and the way to be happy is to make others so.
Robert Green Ingersoll

When I was one-and-twenty
I heard a wise man say,
"Give crowns and pounds and guineas
But not your heart away."

A.E. Housman

Hope is a pleasant acquaintance, but an unsafe friend. Hope is not the man for your banker, though he may do for a traveling companion.

Thomas Chandler Haliburton

Joyful is as joyful does.

There is the path of earthly joy, and there is the path of earthly pleasure. Both attract the soul. Who follows the first comes to good; who follows pleasures reaches not the end.

Upanishads

Why worry about the future? It just came and went.

Walk on a rainbow trail; walk on a trail of song, and all about you will be beauty. There is a way out of every dark mist, over a rainbow trail.

Navajo song

Journeys

The happy person leaves behind their worldly baggage to enter the beautiful hereafter—while the unhappy person adds up the cost of their life and cries over the acquired treasures that they must leave behind.

It is said that he wins who endures
to the end.

**Travel broadens the mind,
and raises the spirits.**

Happiness is along the path that offers
you the chance to find yourself.

He that travels far knows much.

Persian proverb

Be careful what you pretend to be
because that is what you are.

“There’s a light at the end of the tunnel” says the optimist. “It’s probably a train coming straight at us” responds the pessimist.

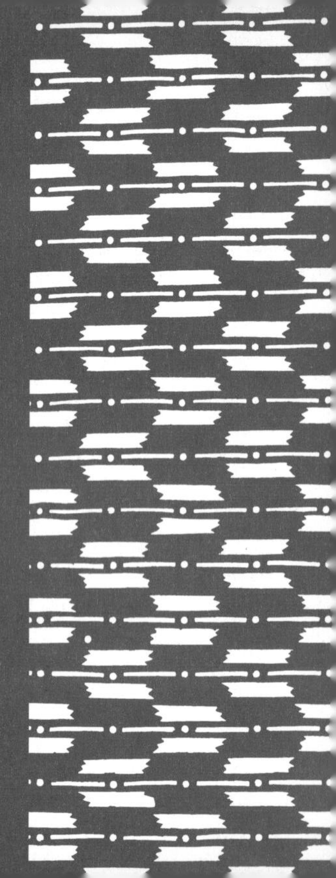

Travel teaches how to see.

African proverb

Happiness is along the path to your own reality, not someone else's.

Think of your life as you do the day—it has light and darkness.

Happiness in where you are and what you do. It is all about choices.

To everything there is a season.

Try to get on the right track and avoid getting run over!

Happiness belongs to those who can realize they are where they want to be.

You can trudge wearily along the well-worn path, or become gloriously lost in the woods that lie on either side.

Seek out all the places where you can be happy—in the city we pine for the country and in the country we long for the city.

You don't have to go anywhere to get somewhere.

Try to recognize your happiness when you arrive at it—don't be like the traveler who doesn't see the valley he is in, only the mountains that surround it.

The world is not a bad place—it's what we're doing to it and in it that causes the problems.

You might not be able to change the world itself on your own, but you can play an important part in changing how we treat it.

The path of error can become the path of truth, if only error is recognized.

Travel light—preconception and prejudice are unnecessary luggage.

Paradise is where you are, paradise lost is where you are not.

Allow commitment toward your path to fuel your determination.

Turn the obstacles on your path into stepping stones.

Let nothing deter you from your happiness—see your path clearly.

Allow yourself to seek out rich and satisfying experiences.

Who can be unhappy in a garden?

The most difficult step of any journey is the first.

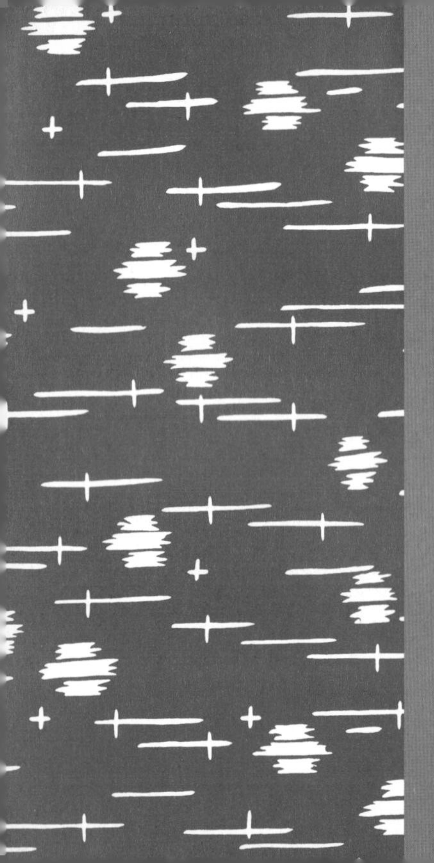

There is beauty at the top of the mountain and in the sunlit plains just as there is beauty in the valley and the deep shadows.

The wise traveler carries their own pack.

I never get to go anywhere he said, standing on the rotating earth.

Avoid the path where nothing blossoms.

Ask yourself whether you are driving away from the garden of Eden.

Where does the journey start?

There is nothing heroic in telling the unhappy of your happiness.

You can try to get to the root of your unhappiness by interpreting your dreams. The explanations of the experts always give you something to laugh at.

Like all of nature, we grow, bloom, and fade. That is our glory and our tragedy.

Life is a journey where the destination is unknown.

All the wonders of the world are within us yet we remain determined to seek them without.

Experience nature—it can bring you boundless energy and great happiness.

The path to happiness is sometimes longer than the path to unhappiness.

It is not the finishing point, but the act of traveling which is important.

A hopeful heart and an open mind are the best traveling companions.

If you are off in search of happiness is your journey really necessary?

Sometimes, like the early adventurers, we feel all at sea—like them we see only the sea and believe, temporarily, that there is no land.

Fortunes come tumbling into some men's laps, others are happy to accept their lot, and others still set out in search of theirs.

All I ask for is the ground beneath me and heaven above me.

Travel only for traveling's sake.

Happiness is not at the destination but in the flowers that you smell along the way.

Just because you take to the sea and cross the world, doesn't guarantee that you will come by treasure.

There are many paths leading to the top of the mountain, but the view is always the same.

On your journeys look out for
the headstone with the inscription:
"Here he lies where he longed
to be."

Standing still doesn't mean
going nowhere.

Don't always be running to
something, or from something.
Sometimes just run.

Where is your secret place—the one
you go to in your hour of pain? Where
a moment's peace can fill your heart.

Allow your mind to settle—like the muddy water churned up by a boat, it will soon become clear when undisturbed.

Be still in a forest. Allow your thoughts to be the only movement in the stillness. Your mind is your power in silence. Listen with your spirit.

Discover your patience. With patience we can bear both good fortune and bad.

There are as many paths as there are travelers.

Each new day has a past, present, and future.There, you see? Things have already moved on.

Until you know yourself there is little point in trying to know others.

Somewhere on your journey don't forget to turn around and enjoy the view.

The pathway to freedom always begins in your own mind.

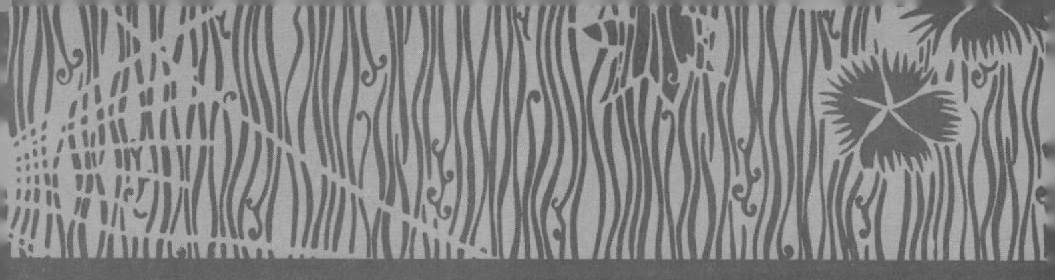

He who runs fastest
doesn't always arrive first.

Love to travel, but do not make the road your home.

One step at a time. And so the most arduous journey is completed.

Enjoy your own company and the depth of your thoughts. How can you ever feel lonely when you've got yourself to keep you company?

Seek inspiration, but see also if you can inspire others along the way.

Respect each moment—it, and your place in it, is unique and never to be repeated.

Journey through your day with efficiency, hope, and a sense of humor.

We should never expect people to be the way we want them to be—honor the integrity of each unique individual.

Use the gift of sight—don't miss a thing and share the joys with others.

The best journeys are not always in straight lines.

Sometimes the most exciting journey you can make is through your own imagination.

Travel in hope, but dwell in happiness.

Travel is the frivolous part of a serious life and the serious part of a frivolous one.

Travel not only with your body, but with your mind.

They often travel furthest that travel nowhere at all.

Part of the path is made up of the mistakes of our lives.

A tree trunk the size of a man grows
from a blade as thin as a hair.
A tower nine stories high is built
from a small heap of earth.
A journey of a thousand miles starts
in front of your feet.

Lao-Tzu

Never think that you have finished learning.

Climb to the top of the boulder that blocks your way, and enjoy the view from a different perspective.

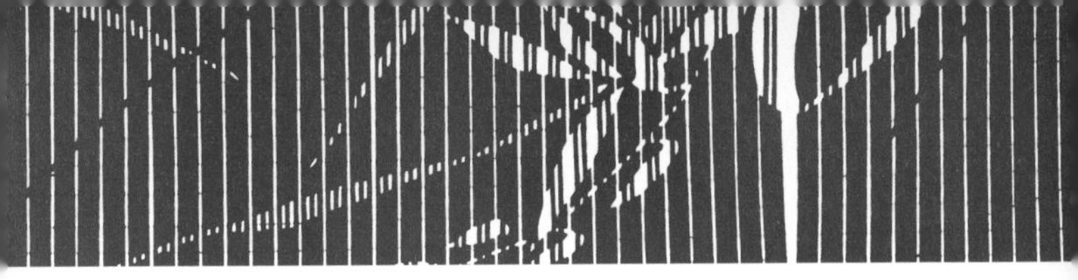

A traveler without observation is a bird without wings.

Saadi

Regrets and recriminations are too heavy a load to bear.

The further your journey takes you, the more dangers you will encounter. The more you dare, the more you win.

The careful foot can walk anywhere.

Chinese proverb

You can travel all over the world, but unless you have a receptive mind you might as well save your fares and stay at home.

Do not imagine the path to happiness as being either long or short.

You must allow yourself the freedom to follow whichever path to happiness you feel is right for you. No two people will choose identical paths.

One must expect to smile and also to weep on the road to happiness.

The path to happiness is a pilgrimage that everyone must make for themselves.

A lifetime of only happiness would be unbearable. It would be its own hell.

Resolve not to be poor: whatever you have, spend less. Poverty is a great enemy to human happiness.

When you can admire without desiring you will know true happiness.

People don't seem to notice whether it's winter or summer when they're happy.

I count myself in nothing else so happy, as in a soul remembering my good friends.

Let a happy song find a path through your sad heart.

Do not expect to find happiness lying on the path waiting for you. Sometimes you have to stray a bit and search in awkward places. Happiness discovered through your own efforts can be doubly rewarding.

You can collect the nuts that have been provided along the way, but you must crack them yourself.

The path must be visited regularly for unused paths soon become choked up with weeds.

Walk too fast or be too impatient and you will miss much.

Along the way there will be thorns but if you look above them you will discover roses.

On your journey, find a handful of things about yourself that you are happy with, and keep them. Find a handful of things about yourself that you are unhappy with, and throw them away.

Once you are able to confront the things that make you unhappy, they will begin to lose their power.

Confront also those things that bring you happiness—not until you are able to acknowledge these will they be free to enter your life.

Don't be so intent upon your own journey that you forget to stop and help others along the way.

Let the happiness you seek be in the here and now, it is no use chasing after memories.

A tree is happy to be a tree even though it has never sat in its own shade. A spoon is happy to be a spoon even though it does not know the taste of soup.

Don’t rely on others to show you the way, carry your own map.

You don’t have to go forward, you can go sideways or upward—just don’t go backward.

There is an ocean, and a forest, and a lane within us all. Places of shade, and light fantastic, and all the time we were seeking to be taken out of ourselves there is a paradise waiting within.

Sacrifice is always necessary. To enjoy the finest vinegar you must make it with your very best wine.

Life is not a race, the winner is not the one who finishes first.

If we could have everything that lay along our path in advance, we might never set out on our journey.

There are those who put so much bait on their hook that no mouth can take it.

He who arrives late is almost always happier than he who has been waiting for him.

If you can admit your unhappiness to those you meet, most will go out of their way to help you find happiness. Do not allow your pride to make you isolated.

Sometimes the road becomes blocked by those who, not realizing that it is there to be crossed, insist upon building their houses on it.

The gardener who was happy to plant the tree he would never see grown provided the shade that keeps us comfortable.

If you lose your way it is better to ask and feel a fool for five minutes than not ask and remain a fool for the rest of your life.

Every time you get frustrated and feel that you're not going anywhere, consider this globe called earth that we are all riding on.

Part of the path is made up of the mistakes of our lives. This route leads to destiny.

The happiest asks directions,
even though he knows the way.

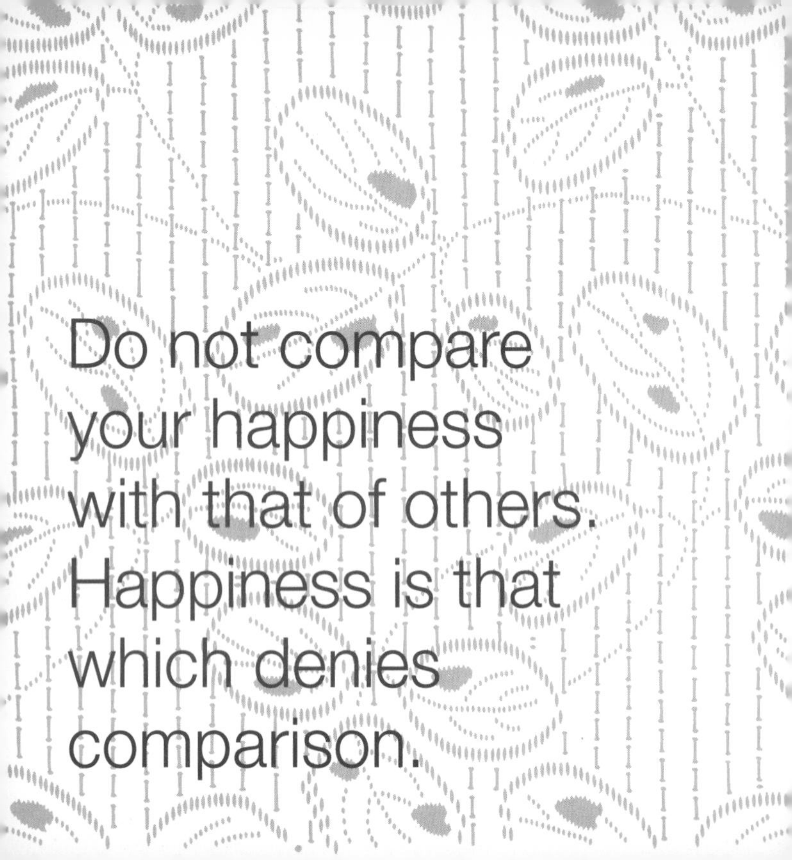
Do not compare
your happiness
with that of others.
Happiness is that
which denies
comparison.

Queries

Why do we so hate being taught when we're so happy to learn?

Why should anyone's desire to be unhappy make anyone else uncomfortable?

Do you suppose there are those among us who weren't made to be happy?

Why is it we seem happy to accept the blame for something, yet we're unhappy about somebody else blaming us?

Happiness doesn't lie in blaming others for your failures. Take responsibiliy for your own actions and your own feelings.

It is not possible to be selfish in practice but not in principle.

Why is the thing we want the most always on the highest shelf?

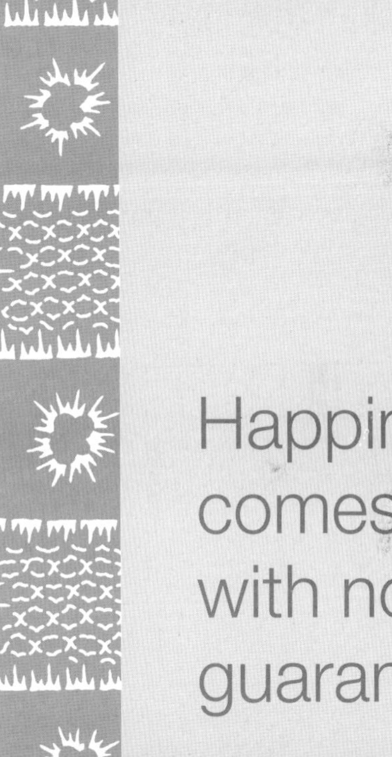

Happiness comes with no guarantees.

Why are
we less
harsh on
others
than we
are on
ourselves?

Why is it so easy to fight for your principles and yet so difficult to live up to them?

Why does the choice between happiness and sadness seem such a hard one to make?

Is there a humble person who isn't proud of the fact?

Is it possible to know why, and how we are happy? If you do, then you truly know happiness.

Happiness is free to the highest bidder.

Do the desires of the heart bring happiness when achieved or would we be happier without those desires?

Why does the first moment of happiness seem to contain everything?

Happiness must be unconditional to be real.

Life is a constant cycle of destruction and healing. Always has been and always will be. The wisest of us are patient whatever the situation and happy in the knowledge that healing or calm will follow.

If I am perfect I have no cracks—so how will I be happy if the sun can't get in?

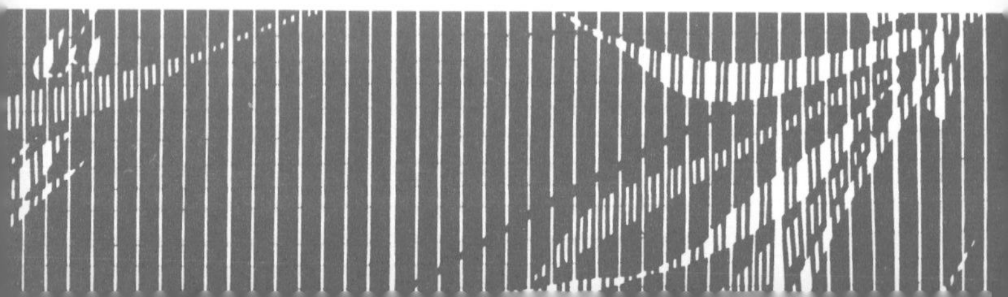

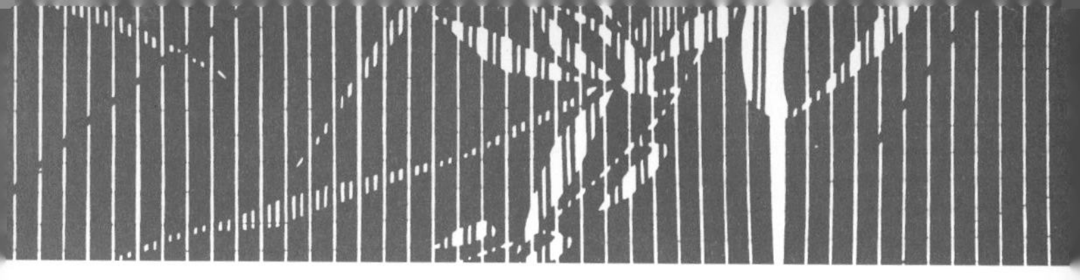

You tell yourself how can you possibly take advantage of what life has to offer if you are not in the right place at the right time. But even in the right place at the right time you can miss your chance.

Why is it that the search for happiness is something that makes so many people depressed?

Is the poor man happier than us because he isn't aware of what we know he lacks?

Even the greatest tyrant looks small from the peak of happiness.

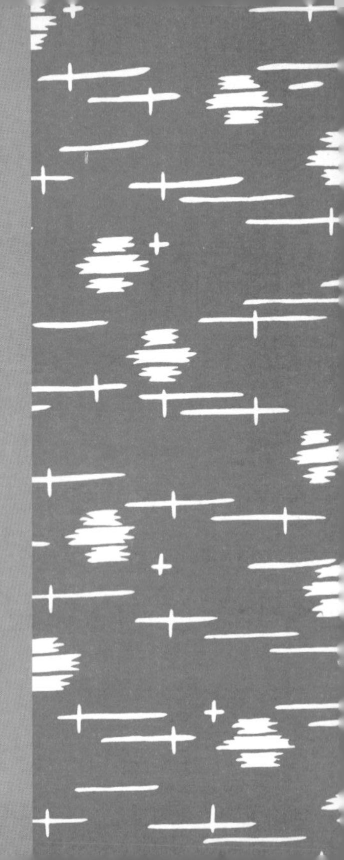

What are we?
Happy.
Where do we come from?
Happiness.
Where are we going?
To greater happiness.

You might be happy about having a doughnut—but what of the hole in its middle?

We seem to want to know if there is life after death? Will it make us happier to know for sure? Even if we don't know what form it takes?

There are those who look forward to the happiness of life after death, and there are those who would prefer a happy life before it.

How can we find happiness if it means letting go of our attachment to suffering and misery?

Are we able to free up all our creative energy to generate a peaceful and happy life?

Could it be that joy is only the shadow cast by sorrow?

Why is it that in order to be happy one must also be concerned with others?

Why is it that we are only allowed by others to be happy if we consent to share our happiness with them?

Does your happiness depend upon internal or external things?

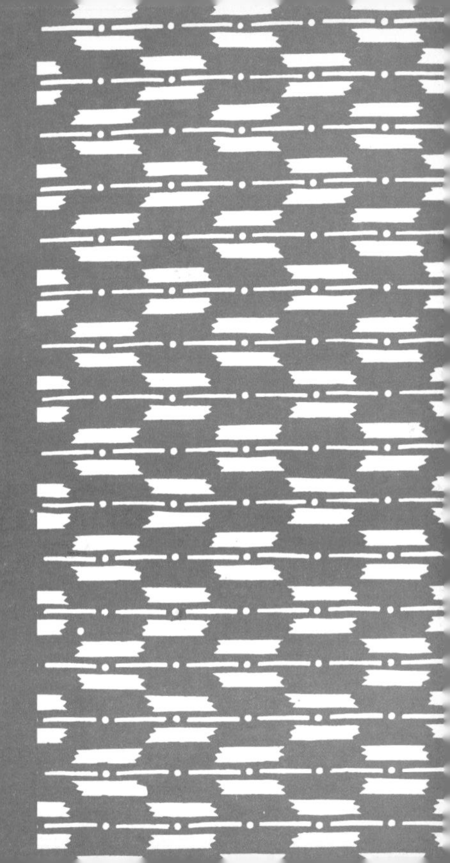

Ask yourself—"Am I happy?" Even if you are you will cease to be so the moment that you ask the question!

Why is the search for happiness often such an unhappy expedition?

Are we ever really as happy or unhappy as we imagine?

Is it possible to be happy and content simply by thinking that you are?

Why is it that when asked why we are happy we become rather like the centipede who was asked by the toad which leg goes after which—she became so distracted she forgot how to run!

Why do we say that we don't mind when it's so obvious that we do?

While half the world wonders what makes the other half happy, half the world is trying to understand the miseries of the other.

How is it that scientists, after a life of research, go to their graves still not understanding what it is that makes us happy?

In order to understand happiness it seems we must first understand ourselves, for that is where true happiness originates and yet we don't seem to understand ourselves in the slightest.

Something akin to happiness rises in my chest every time I complete a task.

How is it that when someone dear to us departs they can take all our happiness with them?

Why is it we assimilate what's pleasing and disregard the rest?

Why does it make us so angry to contemplate being the first to apologize when we'd be happier all the sooner by doing so?

Why is unhappiness considered to be so normal and yet a person who is generally happy considered as being a little bit strange?

Why is it that just thinking about the things that make us depressed can make us so unhappy?

If you are happy to accept help you must also be happy to offer it.

Most of us would like to be remembered for something that made others happy.

What has life taught you? Probably that you'd be happier not knowing how it will end!

Why is it that we are so keen to be remembered after we depart this life, yet we seem unhappy to contemplate what our epitaph will be?

Why is it we seem never content to be happy in love unless it is accompanied by jealousy?

Why is it we seem to be happier asking the harder questions in life and unhappy to ask the simpler ones?

Bang your finger with a hammer. Where does happiness go?

It seems nobody is always happy. Those who love want wisdom, those who are wise seek love, the good are busy seeking power and the powerful want goodness.

Consider your worth in the scheme of things. If there is one thing, no matter how small it is, that you can do better than anyone else, when you cease existing, there will be a gap left unfilled!

No matter how dark our wrongs may seem to us there is always someone prepared to forgive them.

Why do we seem happy enough to ask the meaning of truth then walk away before we get an answer?

The less you know the more you suspect.

The more you know, the more you need to know.

It is an unhappy fact that we are chastized for sloth and praised for study.

Why do we insist on striving for those things we cannot possibly have? What is it that dazzles us so?

Be ready to accept that there is no such thing as the simple truth.

Why should it be that mankind is always in a state of preparing to live instead of actually living?

The thoughts I have thought and the sins I have sinned have all been had before I existed by people I shall never know.

It is impossible to truly understand exactly what it is that makes us happy, so stop trying to figure it out and enjoy the ride!

Why, when given an expensive gift, does a child seem so much happier to play with the box it was packed in?

Expect the best, plan for the worst.

Why is it that some people go through life unhappy yet without an enemy in the world?

The wealthy, it seems, will only be happy if they manage to die beyond their means.

An unused diary can provide as much pleasure as a filled one.

Why is it that in the pain of today we can't have the happiness of yesterday?

The sad man's priceless collection burned in the flames but his colleague's happiest moment remained intact.

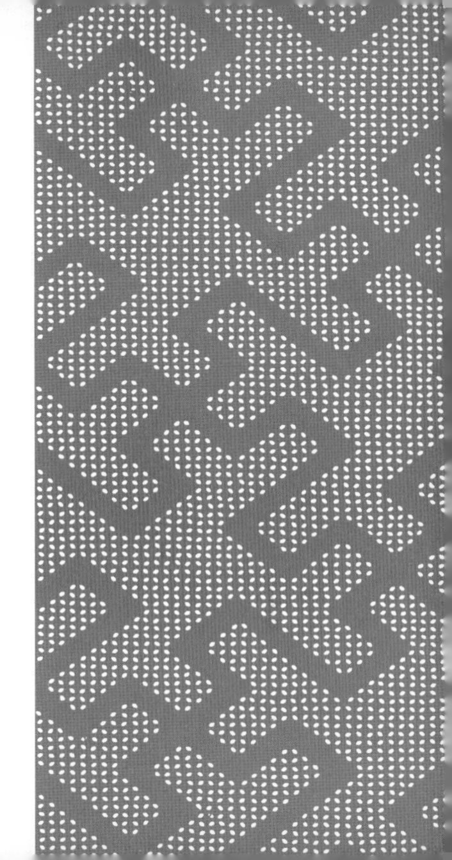

Does happiness come by chance or by creation?

Do you always get what you want and do you always need what you get?

You may be happy to give a coin to charity but are you capable of offering love and showing mercy as well?

Joy and sorrow are opposite sides of the same see-saw.

Are we happy to help people equally?

There is more power in a grain of happiness than grains of sand in a desert.

Happiness comes about by realizing that we all have a unique part to play in the scheme of things.

There are no obstacles in life—only stepping stones of all shapes and sizes.

Why is it we seem incapable of realizing that happiness is not only being able to learn from others but also living in a manner others can learn from?

If you enjoy riddles, then you should enjoy your life.

Why is it that we seem happy to worry when worry solves nothing—to reach happiness the first step should be to stop worrying.

Why do we seem to be happy finding the faults and weaknesses of others?

Being honest with others can make us happy, yet we are often not honest with ourselves.

Are you happy to be one of somebody's problems in life?

Don't waste energy on negative emotions.

Why do we get so unhappy about having too much to do. Look on every challenge as a chance to prove yourself.

Why do so many of us seem happier working to deadlines or under pressure, and yet so many of us suffer from stress?

Why do we seem incapable of facing up to the things that anger us?

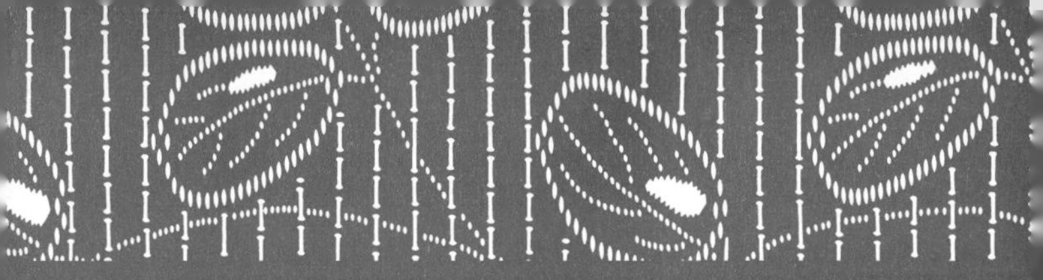

Why is it so difficult to be more assertive?

Why do we allow ourselves to be dogged by time when we'd be happier if we just took the clock down from the wall?

Self-knowledge is the first step toward contentment.

Why should it be that we often feel the joys of others as a personal injury?

Open your eyes to the beauty of the everyday, the mundane, and the ordinary.

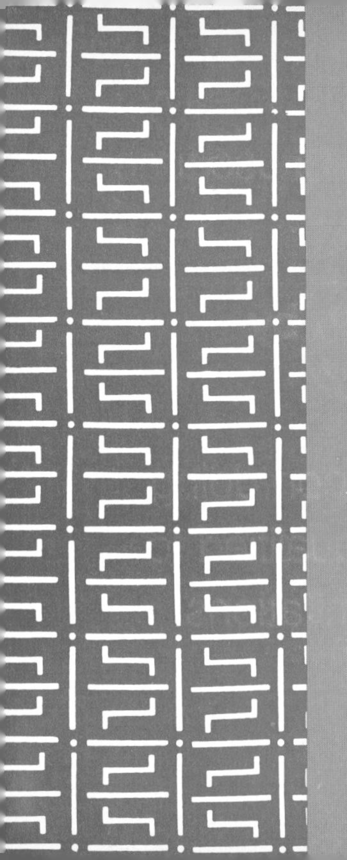

Why do we insist on the same unhappy routine? Sometimes a little change in life can provide happiness—the newspaper you read, the color of your bath towel, a different route to work, or a weekend away by yourself.

Too much freedom is a heavy burden. Learn how to use time effectively.

Why not get happy by getting organized?

Why do we insist upon doing jobs we don't feel qualified to do? Accept your limitations.

Why take on so much work as to feel overburdened?

Why do we let things overwhelm us?

Remember that no thing is greater than the sum of its parts.

Don't resist change, use the opportunity and grow with the situation.

Why, when boredom can be removed by positive thought or action, is it so difficult to make the effort?

If we could enjoy the enjoyable parts of our lives more, then we wouldn't resent the inevitable trials that come our way.

Why not make time for the things in life that make us happy?

Why do we seem unhappy at the thought of relaxing?

Think happy.
Act happy.
Be happy.

Why do we find it so difficult to say no when we would be happier sometimes to do so?

We all have a flow of energy, why don't we work around it?

Why don't we allow ourselves more quality time in order to do the things in life that make us happy?

Why is it that the unhappier we are the unhappier we are about doing physical activities that could make us so much better?

Why are we so unhappy about delegating responsibility when to do so would lead to a happier life?

Happiness should come through feeling in control of time.

Happiness cannot flourish amid the confusion and the clutter of a disorganized life.

If you can't find joy in yourself how can you hope to find it in others?

A smile costs nothing.

Unhappiness is there within all of us and nobody seems to want it.

It shouldn't be so difficult to choose between a smile and a frown.

Why be happy? Who wants to be happy all of the time?

The discovery of a new recipe can do more for the happiness of mankind than the discovery of a new star.

If you are happy to ponder eternity then your happiness will never end.

In youth we are happy for no reason at all—in age we pretend to be happy for millions of reasons.

Published in 2000 by
Sourcebooks, Inc
1935 Brookdale Road, Suite 139
Naperville IL 60563

Design concept: Broadbase
Design: Susannah Good

Printed and bound in China

MQ 10 9 8 7 6 5 4 3 2 1

ISBN: 1-57071-526-2